D0574635

America's Premier Gunmakers

Colt

AMERICA'S PREMIER GUNMAKERS

COLT

K.D. KIRKLAND

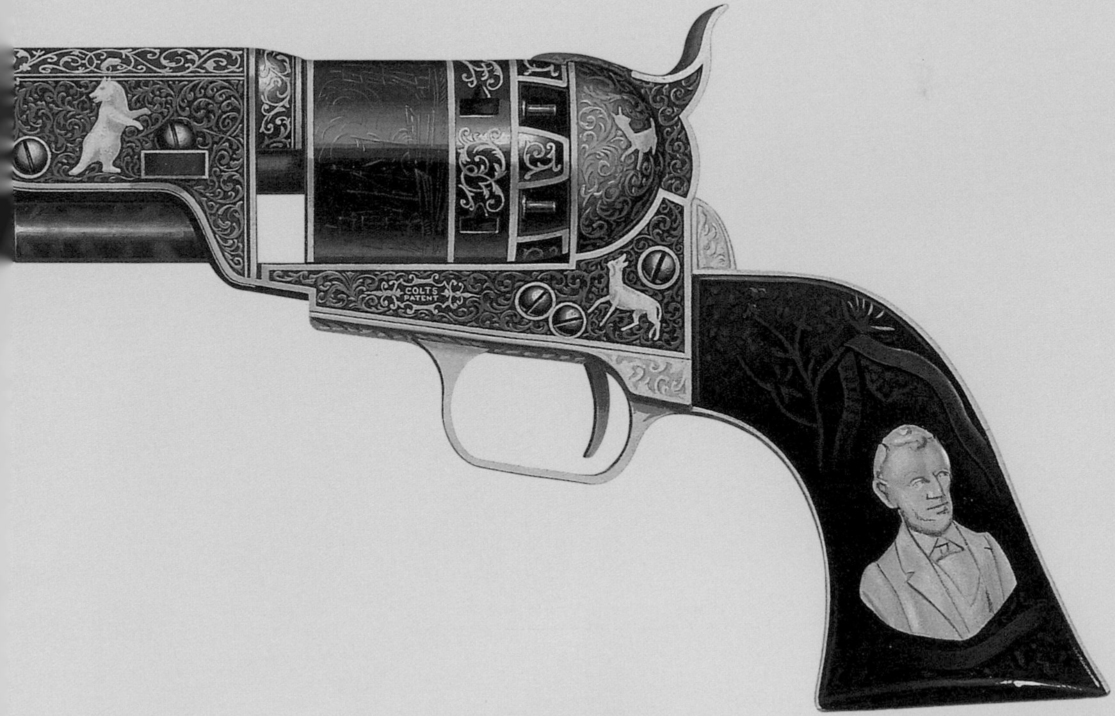

JG PRESS

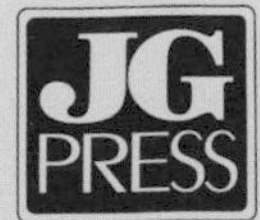

Published by World Publications Group, Inc.
140 Laurel Street
East Bridgewater, MA 02333
www.wrldpub.net

Reprinted 2008 by World Publications Group, Inc.

ISBN 1-57215-102-1
978-1-57215-102-4

Printed and bound in China by
SNP Leefung Printers Limited

Photo Credits

American Graphic Systems Archives 24 (bottom), 28
Prints and Photographs Collection, Barker Texas History Center, University of Texas at Austin 18 (middle)
John Batchelor 2–3 (all), 6–7, 18–19 (top), 26–27, 38–38, 42–43, 46–47, 50–51, 54–55, 58–59, 62–63, 66–67, 74–75, 82–83, 90–91, 98–99, 110–111
Bison Picture Library 106–107
Cinema Shop 44 (right), 47 (top), 84–85, 88–89, 96 (bottom)
Dover 17, 31 (middle)
Ian Hogg 62 (bottom)
Library of Congress 15 (bottom)
National Archives 12 (top), 44 (left)
Peter Newark's Western Americana 62 (middle)
Courtesy of the Royal Artillary Institution, Museum of Artillary at the Rotunda, London Joseph Coughlan 82 (bottom), 108 (bottom)
Seaver Center for Western History Research, Los Angeles County Museum 22–23 (both), 26 (bottom), 30–31, 47 (bottom)
Smithsonian Institution National Anthropological Archives 12 (bottom)
United States Air Force 70, 105 (right)
United States Army 64 (top), 73 (both), 104
John Pinderhughes 103, 109 (bottom left)
United States Department of Defense 65, 74–75 (bottom), 109 (top)
© Bill Yenne 102

Page 1: Samuel Colt, the founder of Colt.

Pages 2-3: Presentation grade firearms: *Upper left:* 1940 Colt hammerless automatic pistol. *Lower left:* Colt Number One Deringer, circa 1870. *At right:* Colt Old Model Navy Percussion Cap revolver.

These pages: Colt Single Action Army Frontier models specially produced by Colt's fine craftsmen for the Texas sesquicentennial.

Table of Contents

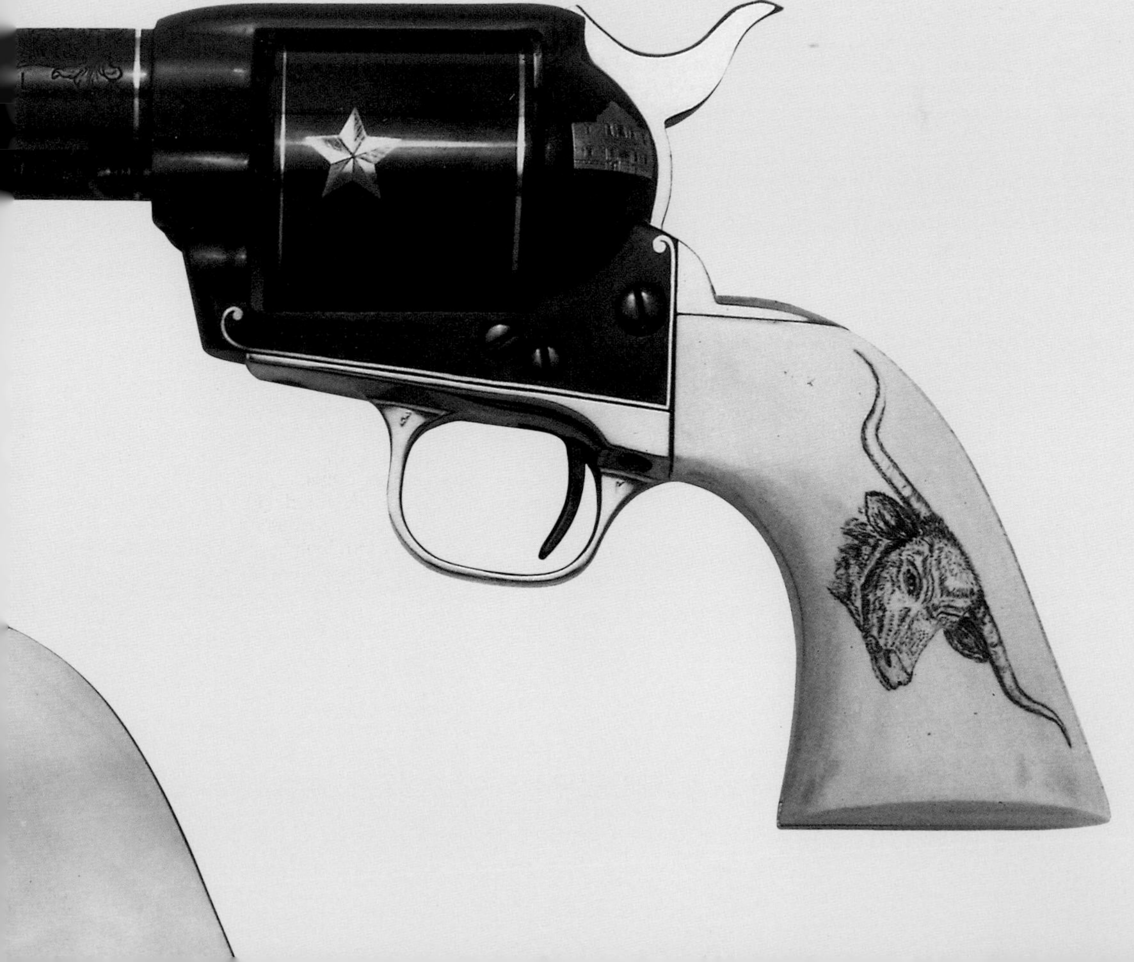

The Arms of

Samuel Colt was born in Hartford, Connecticut on 19 July 1814, the son of Christopher and Sarah Caldwell Colt. Samuel was naturally inquisitive. Apparently, between the ages of seven and 16, he owned several pistols and took them apart to discover the details of their mechanism. Later in life, he attended the Academy of Amherst, but his education there was cut suddenly off—due to his experimentations with torpedo designs, which quickly got him into trouble with the authorities. Samuel's father, Christopher, ran a dye shop. Samuel helped out in the shop and this experience, no doubt, gave him a grounding in chemistry and metallurgy.

On 2 August 1830, Samuel, then a boy of 16, sailed on the ship *Corlo*, bound from Boston to Calcutta, India. It was while on this voyage that Colt, watching the ship's wheel and noting both its rotation and its alignments, conceived the use of the revolving cylinder in a firearm. His concepts were then carved into a wooden model of a pistol resembling the 'pepperbox' type of revolver. On his return, Samuel Colt introduced his idea to Mr Anson Chese, who by trade was a gunsmith. From drawings and the wooden model whittled out on the *Corlo*, an all metal model pistol was produced in 1832.

This first pistol model actually blew up in Colt's hand when he tried to fire it. A new model followed, much improved over the first. That second model contained basically three elements that were to make Colt famous. The three elements were: the rotation of a mini-chambered breech in a single-barreled firearm by the action of cocking the hammer; the locking of the cylinder into place in front of the barrel; and the placing of partitions between the bores of the breech, this to insure that when the pistol fired that only one chamber at a time went off.

Colt had a great idea, but he had no money. At one time his father had been well off, but the family dye business had lost money when Colt was very young—his father could be of no help to him. So in 1832, Colt embarked on a lecture tour of the United States and Canada in which he gave lectures on and demonstrations of nitrous oxide or 'laughing gas.' He knew how to draw an audience, and how to keep their attention, if not their complete sanity. He changed the spelling of his name to Coult and inserted the title Doctor in front of it. This, in combination with the novel nature of nitrous oxide, brought him immediate and considerable success.

These antics with laughing gas were, however, only a part of a larger scheme. Colt never forgot that his prime motivation was money to produce his pistols. Various models were produced in 1832, 1833 and 1834, and finally in 1835, Colt quit the lecture circuit and went to Europe where he took out patents in both England and France for his pistols. He returned to America, and US patents were finally granted him on 25 February 1936.

Based on these patents and the unique designs of these firearms, a new company was formed. The 'Patent Arms Manufacturing Company of Paterson, New Jersey, Colt's Patent' was formed in 1836; $150,000 in stock was sold in order to finance the company, and Colt himself received in payment for his services between one and two dollars for each pistol that was manufactured. This company is referred to in firearms history as the Paterson factory. It commenced its operations with high hopes in 1836, went into bankruptcy in 1841 and closed permanently in 1842. But it was a beginning.

From the Paterson factory came the first promotion model revolver. It was a .40 caliber five shot pistol, with a barrel length of 3.25 inches. This was the first Colt revolver and it was produced in 1835. It is interesting to note that this small gun had a forestock made of wood—to make the gun resemble as closely as possible the standard flintlock guns of its time.

Some interesting methods of determining the number of firearms produced in a factory where no exact records exist are employed by firearms collectors and enthusiasts. A particular model of firearm with a known production number is compared to the firearm without known production num-

Samuel Colt

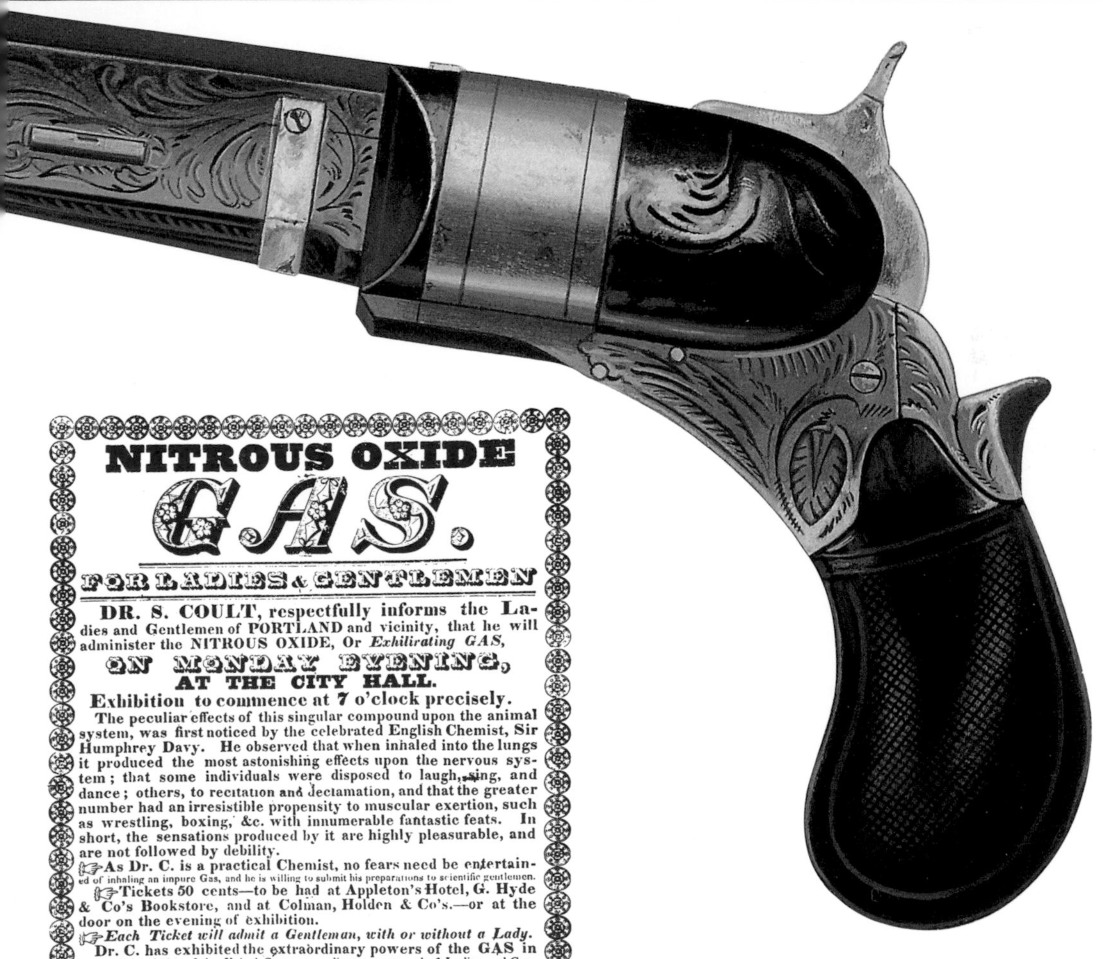

NITROUS OXIDE

GAS.

FOR LADIES & GENTLEMEN

DR. S. COULT, respectfully informs the Ladies and Gentlemen of PORTLAND and vicinity, that he will administer the NITROUS OXIDE, Or *Exhilirating GAS*,

ON MONDAY EVENING,

AT THE CITY HALL.

Exhibition to commence at 7 o'clock precisely.

The peculiar effects of this singular compound upon the animal system, was first noticed by the celebrated English Chemist, Sir Humphrey Davy. He observed that when inhaled into the lungs it produced the most astonishing effects upon the nervous system; that some individuals were disposed to laugh, sing, and dance; others, to recitation and declamation, and that the greater number had an irresistible propensity to muscular exertion, such as wrestling, boxing, &c. with innumerable fantastic feats. In short, the sensations produced by it are highly pleasurable, and are not followed by debility.

☞As Dr. C. is a practical Chemist, no fears need be entertained of inhaling an impure Gas, and he is willing to submit his preparations to scientific gentlemen.

☞Tickets 50 cents—to be had at Appleton's Hotel, G. Hyde & Co's Bookstore, and at Colman, Holden & Co's.—or at the door on the evening of exhibition.

☞*Each Ticket will admit a Gentleman, with or without a Lady.*

Dr. C. has exhibited the extraordinary powers of the GAS in many of the Cities of the United States, to audiences composed of Ladies and Gentlemen of the first respectability—and many Ladies have inhaled the GAS at select Exhibitions. Those Ladies who may be anxious of witnessing the Exhibition, in this city, may be assured, that the City Hall embraces every accommodation for their comfort, and that not a shadow of impropriety attends the Exhibition, to shock the most modest.

He will attend, on reasonable terms, to any applications for private Exhibitions to select parties of Ladies and Gentlemen, if application be made to him at Appleton's, prior to the 16th inst.

☞He will likewise administer the GAS to any gentleman, wishing to inhale it in private, between the hours of 8 and 11, at 50 cents per dose. All persons inhaling the Gas between these hours, have the privilege of admitting two to witness the effects

DOORS OPEN AT HALF PAST SIX O'CLOCK.

PORTLAND, Oct. 13, 1832

Printed at the Argus Office...2 UNION ST.

At left: Lacking money to manufacture his guns, Samuel Colt, posing as the mysterious 'Dr S Coult,' embarked on a series of nitrous oxide demonstrations to raise the necessary cash. This flyer advertises 'Dr Coult's' presentation. *Above:* This is one of the experimental models Colt had made between 1832–1835, before he took out patents and before the Paterson factory was built.

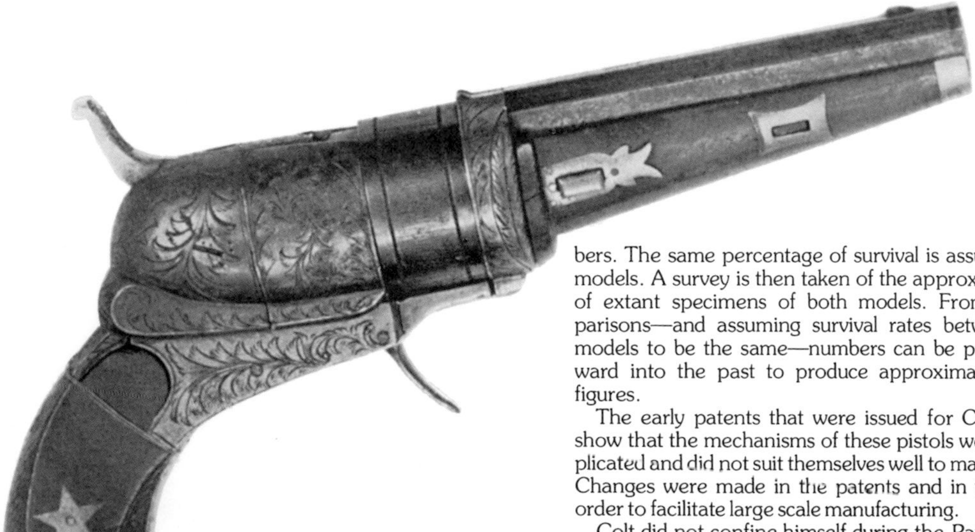

bers. The same percentage of survival is assumed for both models. A survey is then taken of the approximate number of extant specimens of both models. From these comparisons—and assuming survival rates between the two models to be the same—numbers can be projected backward into the past to produce approximate production figures.

The early patents that were issued for Colt's revolvers show that the mechanisms of these pistols were quite complicated and did not suit themselves well to mass production. Changes were made in the patents and in the designs in order to facilitate large scale manufacturing.

Colt did not confine himself during the Paterson factory period to pistols alone. Rifles, carbines, shotguns and even muskets were produced, each having a revolving cylinder. Most of these arms had five-round capacities, with calibers ranging from .28 to .40. Most models employed octagonal barrels.

Many pistols from the Paterson factory were sold in boxes, cloth-lined and wooden in construction. The barrels were of blued finish with stagecoach holdup scenes being

THE UNITED STATES OF AMERICA.

TO ALL TO WHOM THESE LETTERS PATENT SHALL COME:

Whereas SAMUEL COLT, a citizen of the UNITED STATES, hath alleged that he has invented a new and useful improvement in *Fire Arms*, which improvement he states has not been known or used before his application; hath made oath that he does verily believe that he is the true inventor or discoverer of the said improvement; hath paid into the treasury of the United States the sum of thirty dollars, delivered a receipt for the same, and presented a petition to the Secretary of State, signifying a desire of obtaining an exclusive property in the said improvement, and praying that a patent may be granted for that purpose. **These are** therefore to grant, according to law, to the said SAMUEL COLT, his heirs, administrators or assigns, for the term of fourteen years, from the twenty-fifth day of February, one thousand eight hundred and thirty-six, the full and exclusive right and liberty of making, constructing, using and vending to others to be used, the said improvement; a description whereof is given in the words of the said SAMUEL COLT himself, in the schedule hereto annexed, and is made a part of these presents.

IN TESTIMONY WHEREOF, I have caused these Letters to be made Patent, and the Seal of the United States to be hereunto affixed.

GIVEN under my hand at the City of Washington, this twenty-fifth day of February, in the year of our Lord one thousand eight hundred and thirty-six, and of the independence of the United States of America the sixtieth.

ANDREW JACKSON.

BY THE PRESIDENT,

JOHN FORSYTH,

Secretary of State.

CITY OF WASHINGTON, To WIT:

I Do Hereby Certify, That the foregoing Letters Patent were delivered to me on the twenty-fifth day of February, in the year of our Lord one thousand eight hundred and thirty-six, to be examined; that I have examined the same, and find them conformable to law, and I do hereby return the same to the Secretary of State, within fifteen days from the date aforesaid, to wit on this twenty-sixth day of February, in the year aforesaid.

B. F. BUTLER,

Attorney General of the United States.

Above opposite: The Paterson factory, which opened in 1836 and closed in 1842. *Opposite:* This Promotion Model Revolver, made in 1835, was supposed to have been used in selling stock for Colt's new company. *Above:* Preamble to Patent 138, issued on 25 February 1836.

Overleaf: Clockwise from upper left: A patent drawing for Colt's Revolving Gun, patented 25 February 1836; an exploded view of the same; Colt's Revolving Gun designs for (above) pistol and (below) rifle versions; and a view of Colt's cylinder mechanism.

S Colt—Revolving Gun Patent

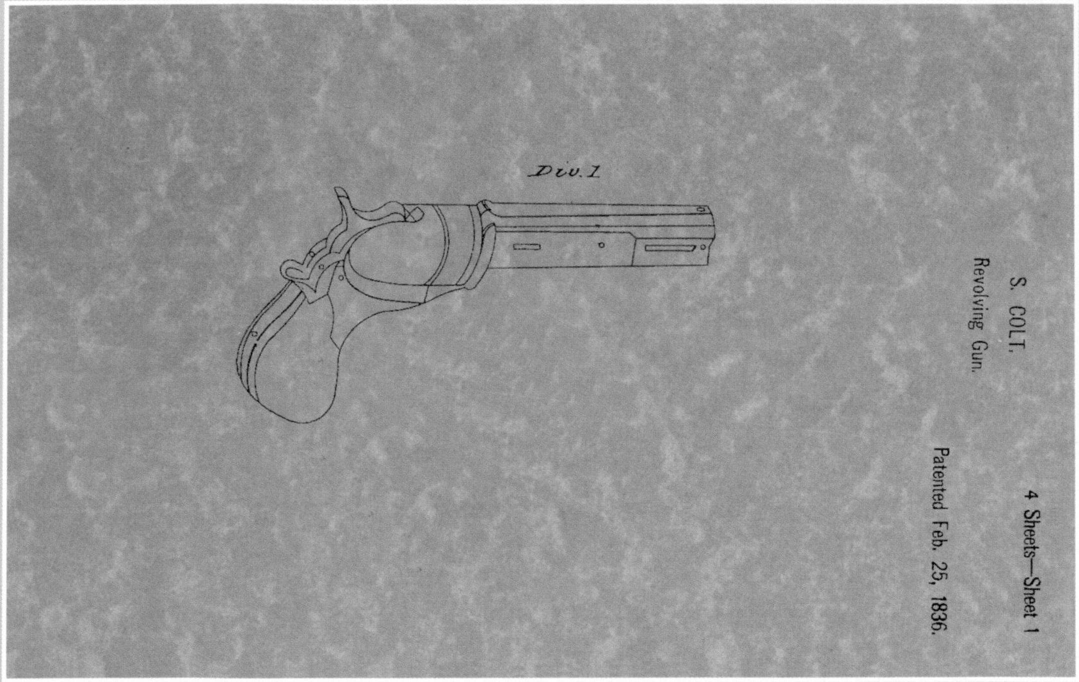
S. COLT.
Revolving Gun.
4 Sheets—Sheet 1
Patented Feb. 25, 1836.

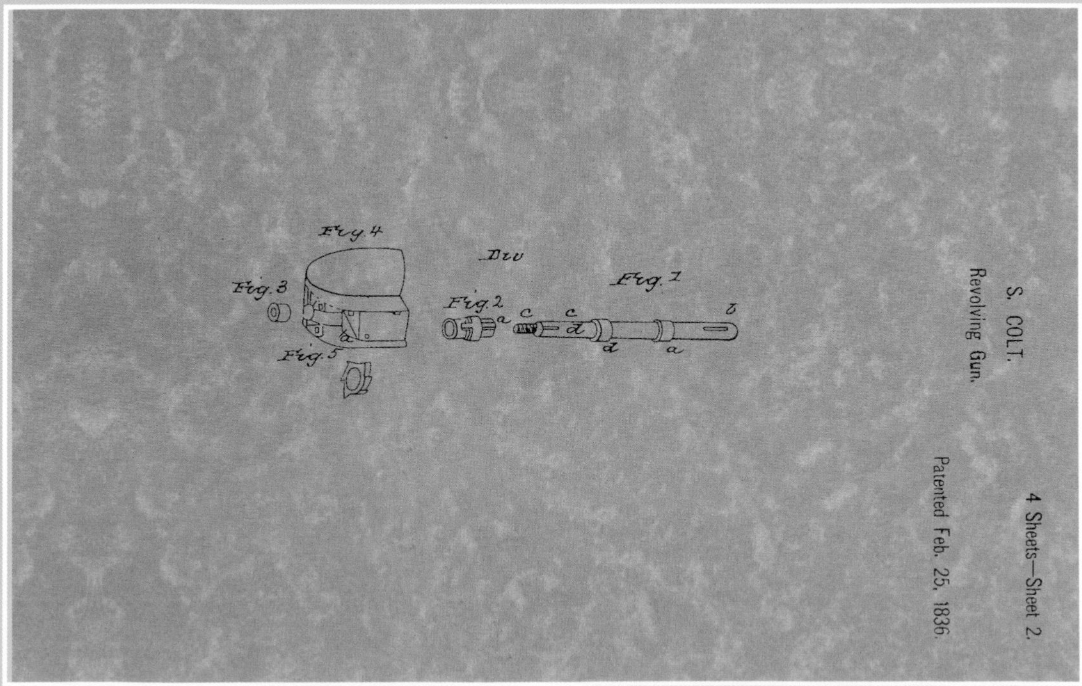
S. COLT.
Revolving Gun.
4 Sheets—Sheet 2.
Patented Feb. 25, 1836.
Fig. 1
Fig. 2
Fig. 3
Fig. 4
Fig. 5

No138, 25Feb1836

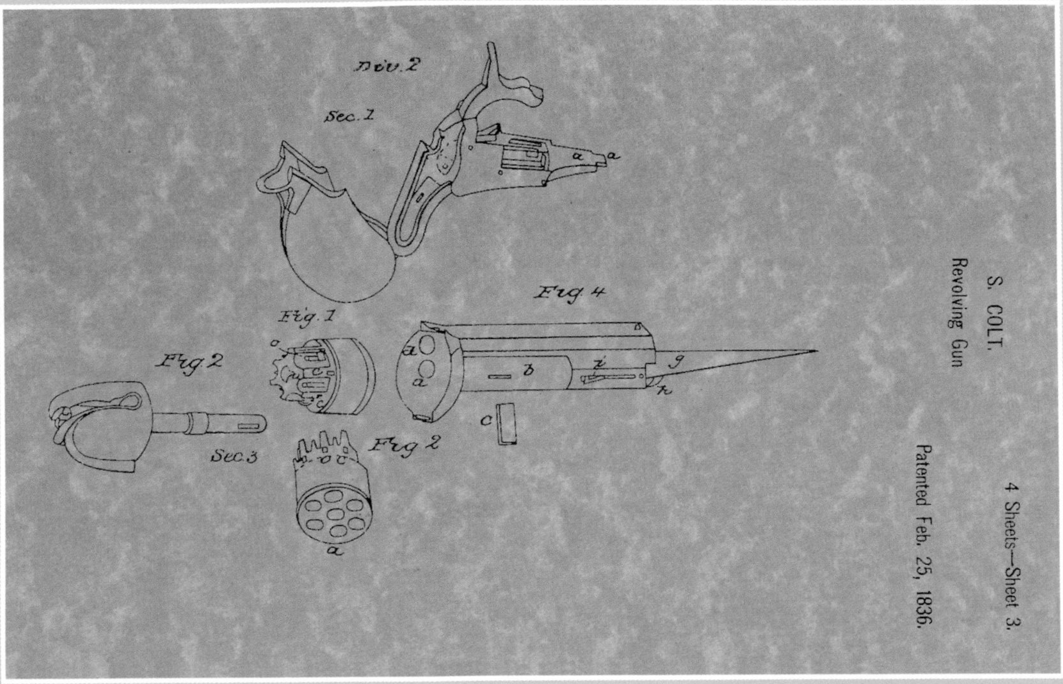
S. COLT.
Revolving Gun
Patented Feb. 25, 1836.
4 Sheets—Sheet 3.
Div. 2
Sec. 1
Fig. 1
Fig. 2
Fig. 4
Sec. 3

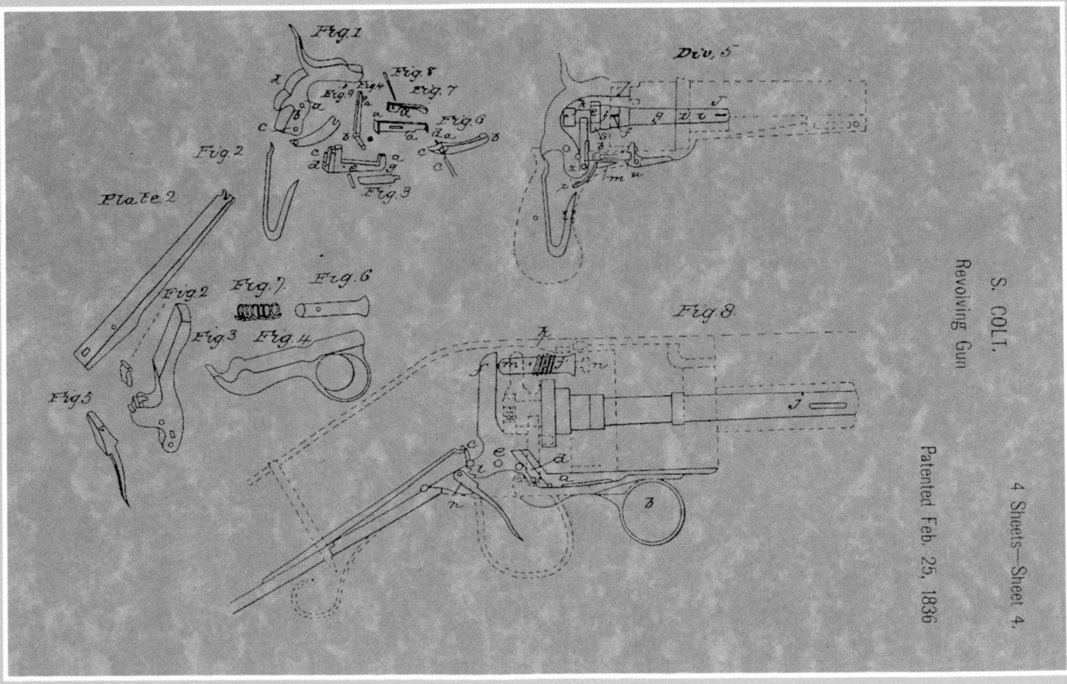
S. COLT.
Revolving Gun
Patented Feb. 25, 1836
4 Sheets—Sheet 4.
Div. 5
Plate. 2
Fig. 1
Fig. 2
Fig. 3
Fig. 4
Fig. 5
Fig. 6
Fig. 7
Fig. 8

Above: **An engraving of the Second Seminole War of 1835,in which Chief Micanopy *(at left)* helped lead the Indians. *At right:* A Paterson Colt cased with accessories. *Below right:* A Paterson Colt and the 1837 Military Pistol. *Bottom right:* The 1837 Paterson Revolving Carbine.**

imprinted in the cylinders. The gun sights were incorporated into the hammer such that when the pistol was cocked and ready for firing, the notch appeared in conjunction with the barrel sight in order to provide aiming capability. A powder flask and magazine-capping device for holding percussion caps were usually included with the boxed pistol, along with a bullet mold, a cleaning rod, and various ingeniously designed tools for disassembling the pistol. Sometimes an extra cylinder was included, thus providing the owner with a total of 10 shots without reloading.

The greatest markets that Colt had for the output of his Paterson Factory were both the South and the Republic of Texas, which at this time was engaged in its war of independence with Mexico. So many of Colt's pistols from the Paterson factory were sold to the Texans that Colt later referred to the regular Paterson model as the 'Texas Arm.'

Even at this early stage, Samuel Colt knew the value of beauty in workmanship and the need for showmanship in the sale of firearms. The Paterson factory was capable of producing special arms, made to order—with differing numbers of shots in the cylinders being available, as well as different kinds of ornamentation. The extravagance of this ornamentation was limited only by the customer's ability to pay for it. It included ornate engravings, inlays and ivory or pearl stocks and handles.

Of course the biggest potential market for firearms was the United States government, and Colt tried in 1837 to get his arms adopted by the government. But government bureaucracy was no less then than what it is today, and Colt was turned down. The Ordnance Board felt that Colt's firearms were too complicated and that therefore they could break down too easily. This, combined with the idea that the flintlock single shot muskets and pistols which were then employed by the army were good enough, led the board to conclude that the status quo was what the government wanted.

But the bureaucrats in Washington were not the men who would actually be using his weapons. So Colt undertook to place his pistols in the hands of soldiers—who he felt would see at once the advantages of being able to deliver several shots without reloading.

Taking a number of his pistols with him, he journeyed to the seat of the Seminole War in Florida, which was the only war going at the time. Here he sold his arms directly to the officers and the troops who were engaged on a day-to-day basis in warfare with the Indians. Naturally, the soldiers in the field found these weapons to be of tremendous advantage over the arms they were accustomed to using. The clamor went up for the government to procure more of Colt's arms. One army captain flatly testified that Colt's firearms were eight times more efficient as arms then in use. Another officer testified that 'if our enemies knew that we were in possession of such arms, they would be less apt to commence hostilities with us.' It was generally felt by those who had used Colt's pistols that one man armed with one Colt pistol was fully equal to five or six men armed with common muskets.

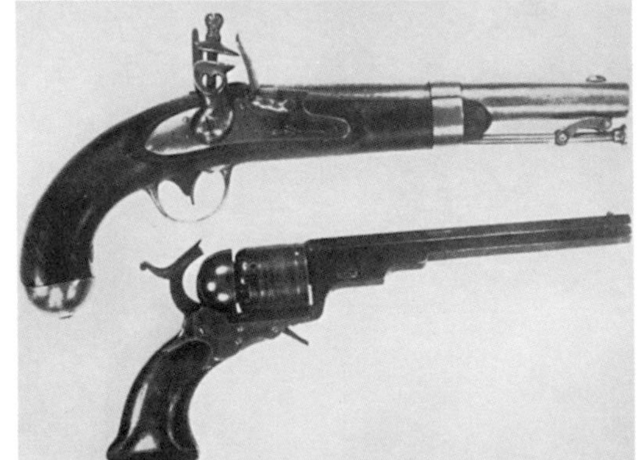

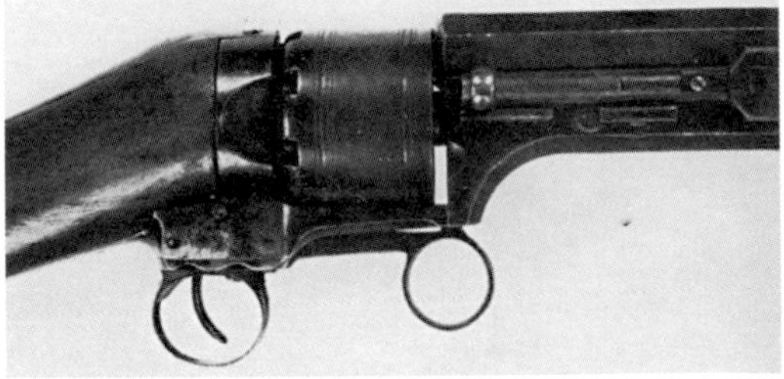

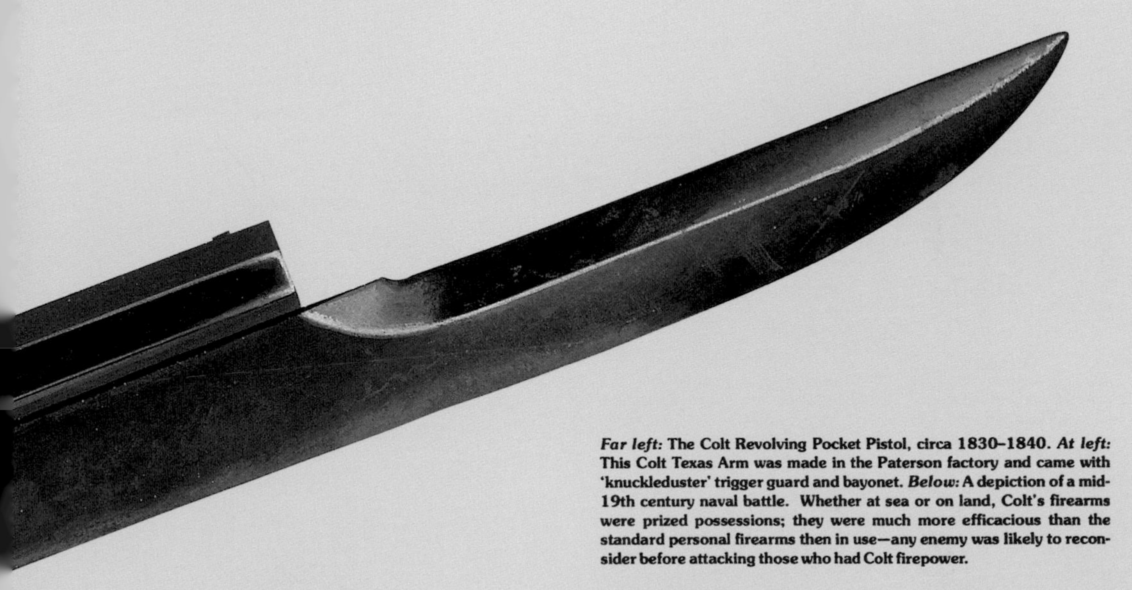

Far left: The Colt Revolving Pocket Pistol, circa 1830–1840. *At left:* This Colt Texas Arm was made in the Paterson factory and came with 'knuckleduster' trigger guard and bayonet. *Below:* A depiction of a mid-19th century naval battle. Whether at sea or on land, Colt's firearms were prized possessions; they were much more efficacious than the standard personal firearms then in use—any enemy was likely to reconsider before attacking those who had Colt firepower.

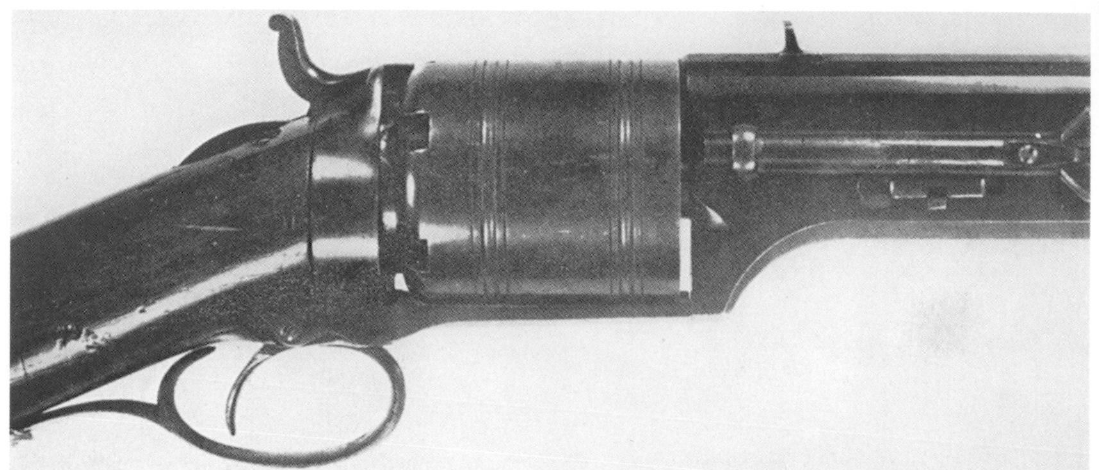

Above: A hammer model of the 1839 Paterson Revolving Rifle (see overleaf caption, page nine). *At right:* An announcement of a demonstration of Colt Paterson arms. *Opposite:* This engraving depicts an 1858 parade, celebrating the laying of the Atlantic Cable, which was presaged by Sam Colt's submarine telegraph cable in New York harbor.

BY CONSENT OF THE MAYOR,

AN EXHIBITION OF

COLT'S PATENT

Repeating Rifles

Will be made at the Battery.

On Monday afternoon, 19th inst.

At half past 4 o'clock.

The public are respectfully invited to attend. The instrument may also be examined at the store of Dick & Holmes, Vendue Range, who have a few of them for sale, price $150 each.

SAMUEL COLT, Patentee.

These Rifles are eight times more effective, and very little more expensive than the ordinary Rifle of equal finish.

DICK & HOLMES, Agents.

February 17th, 1838.

E. C. Councell's print, No. 1 Queen-street.

Unfortunately, while Colt was in Florida selling pistols to men whose lives depended on them, back home his subordinates at the Patent Arms Company were quarreling about management. There are even accounts of some of these employees dueling to the death over their disagreements. Technically, Colt was an employee of the factory, yet it was his ideas and his genius that kept things moving: when he was not personally present, things simply fell apart.

The Paterson Factory came to an end mostly because the guns were sufficiently complicated by design that they had to be made by hand, and that multi-firing arms were not needed by the average man. Time and distance had defeated this first of Colt's factories. It was simply not possible to get enough Colt weapons into the hands of those who needed them and would appreciate them to make the factory profitable. As as result, the 'Patent Arms Manufacturing Company of Paterson, New Jersey, Colt's Patent' closed permanently in 1842.

With the Paterson Factory in bankruptcy, Colt reverted back to (what were for him) his childhood toys—namely, 'torpedoes.' These torpedoes were actually what we would refer to today as mines. Submerged cable, another of his inventions, was used to electrically explode the mine from miles away. In 1842, Congress granted $15,000 for the project, ostensibly to protect US harbors in times of war. Two years later, Congress made a special adjournment to see Colt destroy a ship of over 500 tons, which at that time was under sail and travelling at five knots.

Things submerged intrigued Colt. In the mid-1840s he laid the first underwater telegraph cable in New York harbor.

The year 1845 was pivotal for Colt. Texas had won its independence from Mexico by this time, and had been accepted as a state into the Union. But trouble with Mexico persisted over certain territorial claims in and around the Rio Grande River. General (later President) Zachary Taylor, who had taken part in the Seminole War in Florida, and who may well have been acquainted with Colt's pistols, was sent to southeastern Texas.

As the prospect for hostilities increased, so did the clamor for Colt's repeaters. All the available Colts were purchased by the government and sent to Texas. Now the guns were available to those men who needed them the most. One of those men was Samuel H Walker. Like Taylor, Walker had fought in the Florida wars and had come into contact with Colt's pistols. Walker was a Texas Ranger who, with 14 other men, had at one time engaged 80 Comanche warriors and lived to tell the tale. Their Colt 'five shooters' had allowed them to kill 33 of the marauding Indians.

The supply of available Colts was meager to begin with, and battlefield losses lessened the stockpiles even further. So Walker took leave of the Army in 1846, at Zachary Taylor's order, and came North to both drum up volunteers for the Mexican campaign—and more importantly, to procure more Colt weapons.

Walker got in touch with Colt. The main question was what could be done about getting back into production. Colt possessed his patents only. He had neither money nor a factory. But the world had finally realized the value of his repeaters, and that realization generated a demand that, to this day, survives.

Even though Colt's patents had reverted to him upon the demise of the Paterson Factory, the models he used to produce the guns were lost. But determination was a trait not lacking in Samuel Colt.

He redesigned one of his earlier pistols from memory, even making certain improvements as he went along. These

improvements mainly incorporated fewer moving parts, thus simplifying the process of manufacture and meeting head-on the government's original objections to the pistols as being too unreliable in a battlefield setting.

Walker wanted 1000 pistols as soon as possible. Colt contacted Eli Whitney, son of the inventor of the cotton gin. Whitney was at that time manufacturing arms for the US government in Whitneyville, Connecticut, and agreed to produce the guns, which were to be six, rather than five shot, repeaters and have nine inch barrels. The precision with which Colt's guns had to be made necessitated that Whitney purchase or fabricate special machinery to produce the parts. The total price per pistol was to be $28.00 (this included the accessories).

After the customary barrage of governmental red tape and delays, Colt's pistols began arriving in Mexico. Colt later claimed that because of the contract arrangements with Whitney, he actually made no money on these pistols. When the contract with Whitney expired, however, Colt did wind up owning all of that specialized machinery that the Whitneyville plant used to produce the weapons. And this collection of specialized lathes, dyes, moldings and the like would later provide Colt with the foundation for his Hartford, Connecticut plant.

Colt sent a matched pair of pistols to Walker as a personal present. But shortly afterwards, Walker was killed in action in October 1847. After Walker's death, one of these pistols was sent back to Colt, who regarded it as one of his most

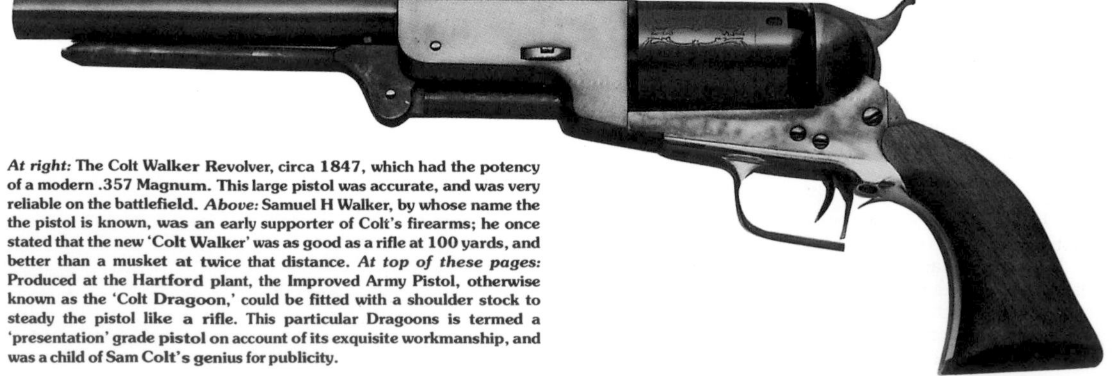

***At right:* The Colt Walker Revolver, circa 1847, which had the potency of a modern .357 Magnum. This large pistol was accurate, and was very reliable on the battlefield. *Above:* Samuel H Walker, by whose name the the pistol is known, was an early supporter of Colt's firearms; he once stated that the new 'Colt Walker' was as good as a rifle at 100 yards, and better than a musket at twice that distance. *At top of these pages:* Produced at the Hartford plant, the Improved Army Pistol, otherwise known as the 'Colt Dragoon,' could be fitted with a shoulder stock to steady the pistol like a rifle. This particular Dragoons is termed a 'presentation' grade pistol on account of its exquisite workmanship, and was a child of Sam Colt's genius for publicity.**

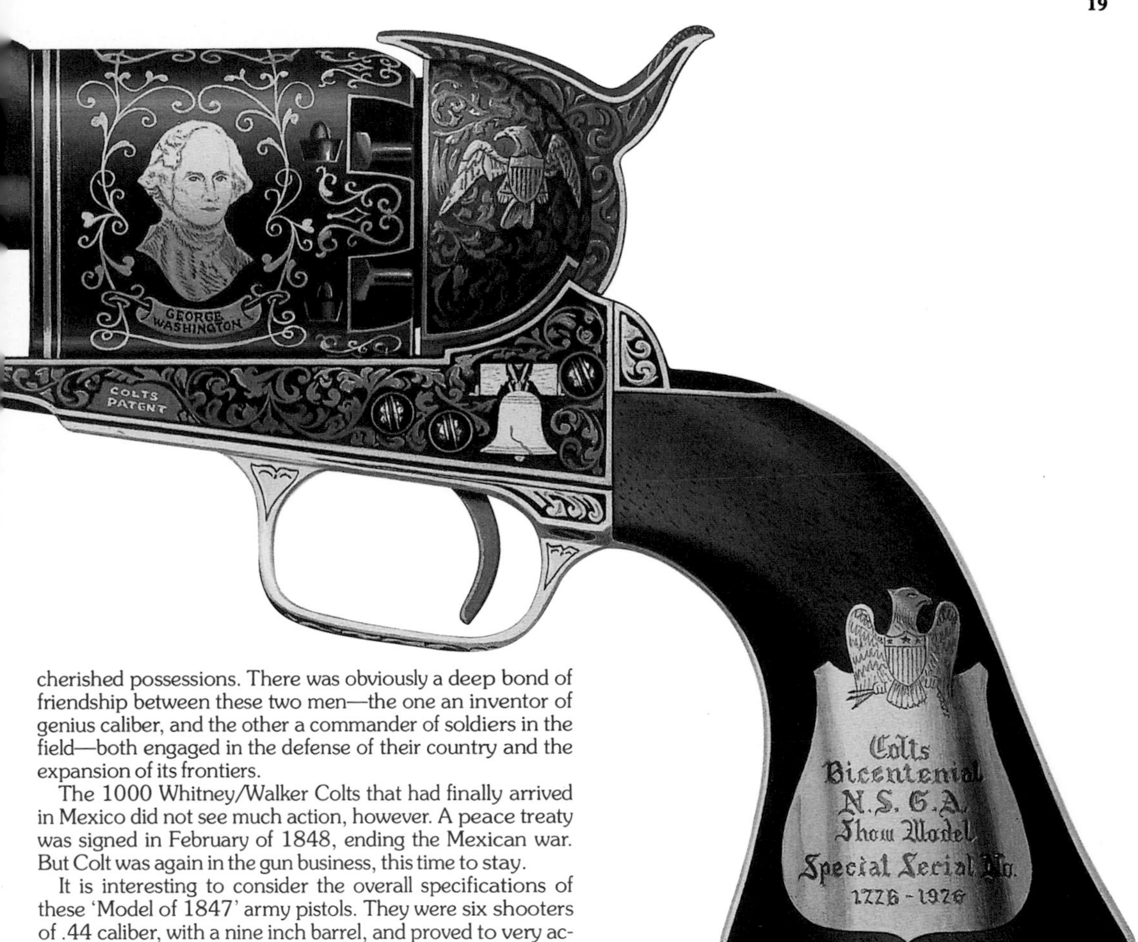

cherished possessions. There was obviously a deep bond of friendship between these two men—the one an inventor of genius caliber, and the other a commander of soldiers in the field—both engaged in the defense of their country and the expansion of its frontiers.

The 1000 Whitney/Walker Colts that had finally arrived in Mexico did not see much action, however. A peace treaty was signed in February of 1848, ending the Mexican war. But Colt was again in the gun business, this time to stay.

It is interesting to consider the overall specifications of these 'Model of 1847' army pistols. They were six shooters of .44 caliber, with a nine inch barrel, and proved to very accurate indeed. Walker stated them to be as good as a rifle at 100 yards, and better than a musket at twice that distance. They weighed four pounds, nine ounces, and displayed the now famous squareback triggerguards made of brass. In firepower, they were about equal to today's .357 Magnums. Quite an achievement for the 1840s! In addition, honoring the man who inspired, in a sense, the design of these pistols, this model is commonly known as the 'Colt Walker.'

Samuel Colt was by nature a showman. He turned this flair for catching the public mind to his advantage by starting the practice of making 'presentation' grade, usually boxed, sets of pistols to give as gifts to powerful and influential people. These specimens were often masterpieces of the gunmaker's art. They were virtually flawless in appearance. Deep bluing was set off by heavy inlays of polished gold flowing over the barrel and other parts in delicate traceries. The grips were often richly carved with ivory insets. Who would not have been (or would not be today) stunned by such a noble gift?

It was at his factory on Pearl Street in Hartford that the large scale production of Colt pistols began. Between the years 1845 and 1852, an average of 1000 firearms per year were produced by the Hartford Factory, including carbines as well as repeating pistols. Times were changing, and the need for firearms was growing. The Gold Rush to California was under way. Pioneers were pushing westward. A general feeling of lawlessness had engulfed the nation, and the need for personal protection had grown. Colt was very aware of these circumstances, and quickly added pocket pistols and belt models to his line of firearms.

One of the most interesting pistols to be produced at the Hartford Factory was the Improved Army Pistol, which is called by collectors the 'Colt Dragoon.' These Dragoons were six shooters of .44 caliber, and were made in both 7.5 and eight inch barrel lengths. The Colt Dragoon was the mainstay of the pistol line until it was superseded by the New Model Army Pistol in 1860.

It is interesting to note that the Dragoons, when sold to both the army and civilians, could be equipped with shoulder stocks that could, in effect, turn the pistol into a rifle. This was feasible because of the overwhelming advantage of accuracy that the Colt weapons possessed in relationship to other weapons of the day. From 1847 until 1860, the total production of Colt Dragoons was about 22,000, and apparently half of these went to civilians.

As the popularity of his guns increased, so did the probability of patent infringements upon Colt's designs. Colt took to imprinting upon each of his firearms 'Colt's Patent,'

Above: The Whitneyville Armory, where the Whitneyville Colts were made in 1847. _At right:_ Part of the original Hartford, Connecticut plant. From this small beginning, the plant expanded on a grand scale _(below right)_: at this stage, the factory was shaped like the letter 'H,' and its entrance was capped by a blue dome covered with gold stars.

and in his advertising the words 'Beware of counterfeits and patent infringements' appeared regularly.

Even though the original Dragoons were of the cap and ball variety, they proved to be extremely popular even after the invention of the center fire cartridge. And in the middle 1970s, 100 years later, Colt Arms bowed to this continuing demand by producing the 'Third Model Dragoon.'

In 1848, Colt so perfected the designs of his weapons, and particularly the Dragoons, that the parts of all of the arms of the same model could be interchanged with parts from other Colts. Again, this was due to the standardization of measurements and the perfecting of the precision of the machinery on which the arms were produced. The simplification of manufacture produced only five moving parts in the Dragoons, as opposed to 17 such parts in earlier models.

There are three basic classifications of Dragoon pistols which are used by collectors today. The Number One Dragoon is the first model that was made at Hartford, and incorporated a round cylinder, square back trigger guard and no roller on the hammer.

The Number Two Dragoon was an improved model that was made after 1849. It featured a round back trigger guard, rectangular cylinder notches, a roller on the hammer and pins between the nipples. The Number Three Dragoon is virtually the same as the Number Two, except that it is fitted with a shoulder stock.

Colt's master patent was granted him by the United States government in 1836 and was due to expire by 1849. But the legal reasoning behind the granting of patents was that a patent was to be issued so that the inventor could have a sufficient amount of time in which to tool up and produce his invention free of competition and, thereby, realize a profit on his idea. Colt, however, was able to prove that he had *not* received a reasonable profit in the 14 years since the patent was issued, and an extension was granted him until 1857.

By the early 1850s, Samuel Colt was a prosperous and influential figure. He was given a commission as a lieutenant colonel in the Connecticut State Militia. Thereafter he referred to himself, rightfully, as Colonel Colt. It is interesting to note, however, that in 1861 the Colonel's official military commission was withdrawn. This was due to the fact that he was far more valuable to his country as an arms inventor and producer than he was as a field commander.

In June of 1856, Samuel Colt married Elizabeth Hart Jarvis. Her brother was vice-president of the Colt Armory at that time. The couple honeymooned in Europe for six months and even attended the coronation of Tsar Alexander II in St Petersburg, Russia. In 1858, Colt sent three sets of firearms engraved and inscribed to the new Tsar. These guns are, by far, the most intricate of the presentation models and presently reside at the Hermitage Museum in Leningrad in the Soviet Union.

The Hartford Plant grew on a grand scale. The main factory building itself was of brick construction and shaped like the letter 'H.' It was three and one half stories high and each parallel section of the 'H' was 500 feet long. The building itself was capped by a large blue dome containing gold stars similar to a Russian Orthodox cathedral.

The Hartford Factory developed into a school of great influence for inventors, technicians and mechanics of the day. Colt's magnetic personality drew many of the best minds in the United States to him. Rollin White at one time worked for Colt and himself patented certain devices which later became the basis for the Smith and Wesson Firearms Company. Francis A Pratt and Amos Whitney were associated with Colt during this period and their partnership later formed the Pratt and Whitney Company, which today manufactures engines of almost every kind.

In 1850, two models of pistols were introduced by Colt. The Model 1849 Pocket Pistol and the Model 1851 Navy Pistol came to the marketplace. Since there is a series of belt and pocket pistols associated with this period of time, it is well to quote from Colt's *Armsmear* publication to differentiate the models involved. 'Pocket Revolvers' with six inch, five inch, four inch and three inch barrels and .31 bore, were introduced about 1848. They were first made without lever rammers and were loaded by removing the cylinder from its pin and using the pin for a rammer.

FYLER
PRODUCTS
INC.
DAIRY and
POULTRY
SUPPLIES
FYLER
CHEMICAL & SUPPLY CO.
HARTFORD, CONN.
GROVE
AUTO CLEANING
INSIDE STORAGE 6
YARD PARKING
DAY PARKING 10¢

At right: **A prime example of a First Model Hartford Dragoon, circa 1846, with the squarebacked triggerguard typical of the early Colt dragoons.** ***Below right:*** **An Old Model Pocket Pistol of 1850.** ***Opposite:*** **An early 1850s Colt advertisement, showing a Colt Dragoon—as assembled and as disassembled.**

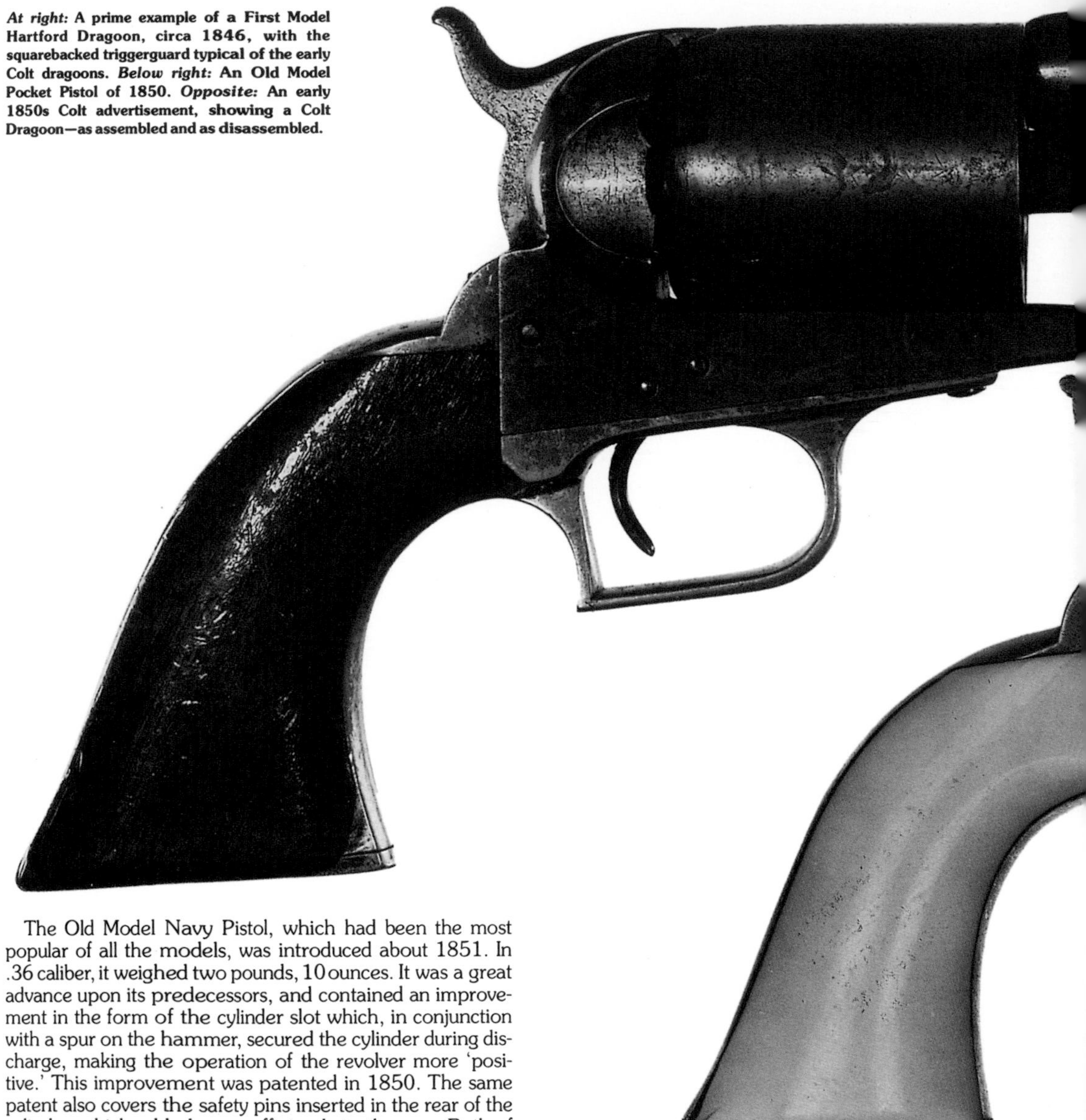

The Old Model Navy Pistol, which had been the most popular of all the models, was introduced about 1851. In .36 caliber, it weighed two pounds, 10 ounces. It was a great advance upon its predecessors, and contained an improvement in the form of the cylinder slot which, in conjunction with a spur on the hammer, secured the cylinder during discharge, making the operation of the revolver more 'positive.' This improvement was patented in 1850. The same patent also covers the safety pins inserted in the rear of the cylinder, which added more efficiently to the arm. Both of these improvements have been retained in nearly all the Colt revolvers made since.

The Old Model Pocket Pistol was improved in 1849 by the introduction of the improved features of the Navy Pistols and has not been materially altered since. It was .31 caliber, and its weight was from 24 to 27 ounces, dependent upon the length of its barrel.

The New Pocket and New Model Police, New Model Army and New Model Navy, were all introduced after 1860. They presented nothing new in principle, but by a better arrangement of parts—and in the Army Model, by less weight—suited the markets better, and were mostly made in .36 caliber, except for the New Model Army in .44 caliber.

The New Pocket Pistol weighed from 25 to 28 ounces, the New Model Police Pistol weighed from 24 1/2 to 26 ounces, the New Model Navy Pistol weighed two pounds 10 ounces, and the New Model Army Pistol weighed two pounds 11 ounces.

Also, during this period, the Sidehammer series of guns was introduced. The thing that made the Sidehammer series unique was that for the first time, a solid frame was employed. This means that the barrel was screwed into the frame, thus making the barrel and frame integral.

It is interesting to note that even on common production

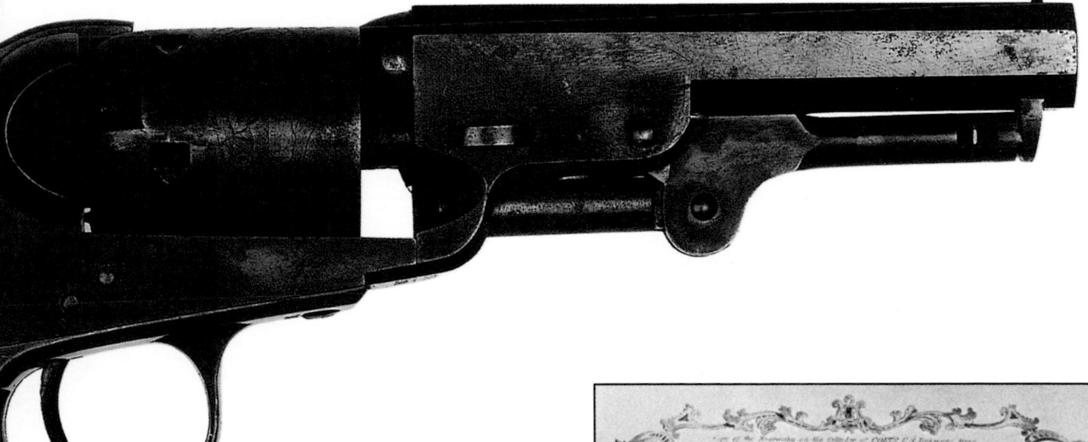

models, the scene that appeared on the cylinders was usually of a fight between pistol-armed men and Indians. Later, these cylinder scenes would change. On the cylinders of the Navy Colts, the scene was generally one of both steam and sailing ships battling one another. The overall motif for these naval battle scenes was taken from an episode in the Texas War of Independence in which Commodore Moore of the Texas Navy defeated a fleet of Mexican vessels which was greatly superior to his own fleet: this actual historical event was used to demonstrate the fact that a man armed with a Colt could defeat a force vastly outnumbering him.

The 1851 Navy Colt was very popular as a belt revolver, because it was lighter than the Dragoon. The Navy Pistol, which was actually used by the Army (and comparatively little by the US Navy), wound up being a favorite dueling weapon among various adversaries in the California Gold Rush period.

In 1849, Colt hired a Mr EK Root as his factory foreman and general superintendent. Root was a mechanical engineer and inventor in his own right. But his talents did not come cheaply. Colt exhibited a fair amount of farsighted wisdom by hiring Mr Root at the price demanded. Colt felt—and was later justified in believing—that it was cheaper, in

Clockwise from immediate above: **The sidearms worn by these cowpokes in this 1927 photo are Colts, underscoring Colt's continued popularity; an Old Model Navy Pistol with shoulder stock; an Old Model Army Pistol, also equipped with a shoulder stock; the Colt London factory, at which the 1849 Model Pocket Pistol and the 1851 Navy Pistol were made; and a pamphlet advertising Colt's London models.**

the long run, to hire expensive men than to hire cheap ones of lesser talents. Indeed, this kind of thinking led Colt to pay his better class workmen $5.00 a day, which at that time was roughly five times the going rate for such labor. But when high wages are paid, high demands can be made and the workers and management at the Hartford Plant lived up to all expectations. Arms were produced rapidly and efficiently. Marketing and advertising schemes, principally under Colt's direction, increased the reputation of Colt's firearms and his markets and orders grew at an astonishing rate.

The United States was not the only nation involved in conflict. This Colt knew and on foreign trips he managed to come in contact with heads of state then involved in regional wars. One such foreign leader was the Sultan of Turkey. Colt presented him with a pair of presentational revolvers, which led the Sultan to immediately order 5000 such arms and make to Colt a personal present of a jewel encrusted gold snuffbox. Later, Colt was to be the recipient of an Order of Turkish Nobility decoration from this same sultan.

Even though the designation 'Colt's Patent' appeared on Colt's firearms, there were always those ready to imitate the genuine article for their own profit. Fortunately, Colt was now wealthy enough to employ a battery of lawyers, who pursued these patent infringements vigorously. Colt's patents basically incorporated three principles in revolver construction: 1) turning the cylinder by the action of cocking the hammer, 2) locking and unlocking the cylinder by the same action of cocking and 3) providing a block between the chambers to prevent simultaneous discharge of several chambers. The infringers always lost and as long as Colt's patent remained intact, they had to search elsewhere for designs.

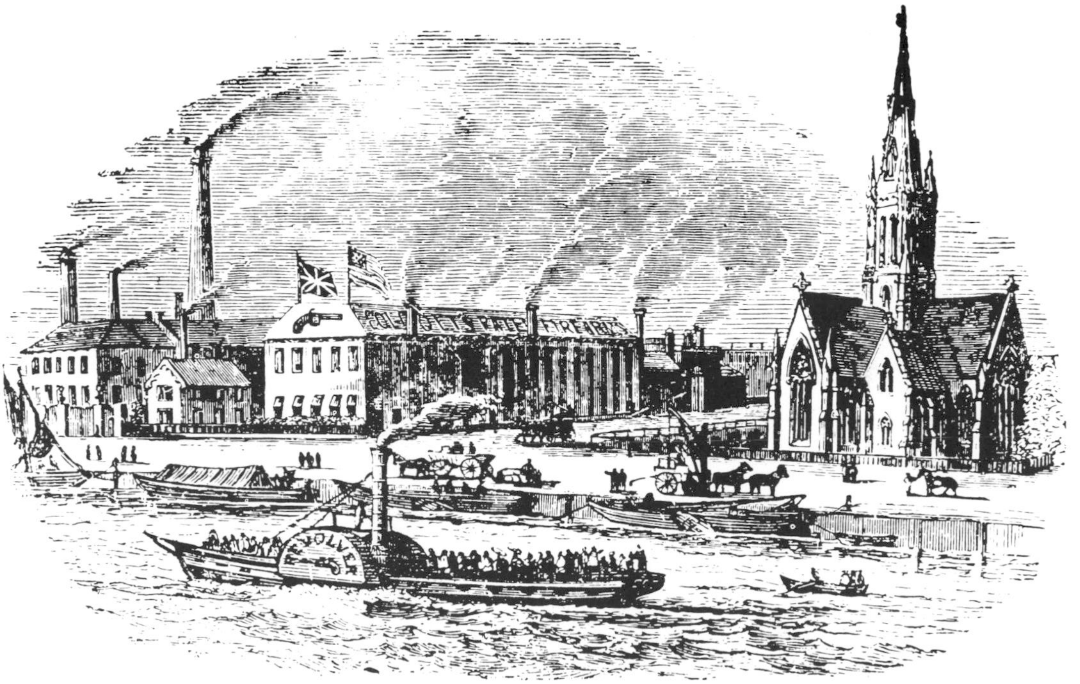

In 1851, Colt had gone to Europe and had given a series of lectures before the Institute of Civil Engineers at London. These lectures and the ensuing discussions turned into a litany of praise for Colt and his new pistols. The British, at this time, being 'the rulers of the world' had ample need for the latest in weaponry in order to quash the local uprisings, disturbances and disputes that almost continually plagued the Empire.

Colt set up a pistol factory in London in 1853 in order to exploit this market. It was situated at Pimlico on the Thames Bank near Zaruxall Bridge. The arms models made here were the 1849 Model Pocket Pistol and the 1851 Navy Pistol.

Since gunmaking in the British Isles at this time was mainly a piecemeal project, whereby a gun was produced in many different locations—usually backstreet workshops—the London Colt Factory was the source of great amazement to English observers. Not only were all of Colt's guns made under one roof, but the machinery used was of such perfection and precision that it could be run by women whose only former training had been in needlework. The London Factory was all the rage for British society and even Charles Dickens wrote of his tour through it in *Household Words* in 1855.

COLT'S PATENT REPEATING PISTOLS,

ARMY, NAVY, AND POCKET SIZES,

APPROVED OF BY HER MAJESTY'S HON. BOARD OF ORDNANCE, AND THE MOST DISTINGUISHED NAVAL AND MILITARY AUTHORITIES,

AND NOW IN GENERAL USE THROUGHOUT THE WORLD.

MANUFACTURED AT

THAMES BANK, NEAR VAUXHALL BRIDGE;

OFFICES FOR SALE OF ARMS, 1, SPRING GARDENS, COCKSPUR STREET, LONDON.

BEWARE OF COUNTERFEITS AND PATENT INFRINGEMENTS.

Every genuine London-made Weapon is stamped on the barrel—" Address, Col. Colt, London."

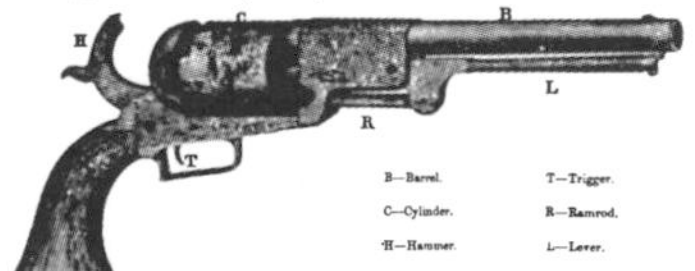

DIRECTIONS FOR LOADING COLT'S PISTOLS.

First explode a cap on each nipple to clear them from oil or dust, then draw back the hammer to the half-cock, which allows the cylinder to be rotated; a charge of powder is then placed in each chamber, and a ball with the pointed end upwards, without wadding or patch, is put one at a time into the mouths of the chambers, turned under the rammer, and forced down with the lever below the surface of the cylinder, so that they cannot hinder its rotation. This is repeated until all the chambers are loaded. Percussion-caps are then placed on the nipples, when, by drawing back the hammer to the full-cock, the arm is in condition for a discharge by pulling the trigger; a repetition of the same motion produces the like results, viz. six shots without reloading. ☞ The Hammer when at full-cock, forms the sight by which aim is taken.

To carry the arms safely when loaded, the hammer should be let down on one of the pins between each nipple, on the end of the cylinder.

The arm should be thoroughly cleaned and oiled after firing, particularly the base-pin on which the cylinder turns.

Soft lead must be used for the balls. The cylinder is not to be taken off when loaded.

THE QUANTITY OF POWDER USED FOR THE DIFFERENT SIZE PISTOLS.

Cavalry or Holster Pistol	. . .	1[illegible],	1[illegible]	or	1[illegible] drachm.	Fine-grain Powder the best.
Navy or Belt	ditto (second size)	[illegible],	[illegible]	or	[illegible] ditto	
Pocket	ditto (4, 5, and 6 inch barrel)	[illegible],	[illegible]	or	[illegible] ditto	

N.B.—It will be safe to use all the Powder the chambers will hold, leaving room for the Ball, whether the Powder is strong or weak.

DIRECTIONS FOR CLEANING.

You must set the lock at half-cock; then drive out the key that holds the barrel and cylinder to the lock-frame—they can be removed; should the barrel stick on the base-pin, the lever may be used to aid in removing it, by forcing the rammer on the partition between the chambers. Take out the nipples. Wash the cylinder and barrel in warm water, dry and oil them thoroughly; oil freely the base-pin on which the cylinder revolves.

TO TAKE THE LOCK TO PIECES, CLEAN, AND OIL.

First—Remove the stock, by turning out the bottom and two rear screws that fasten it to the guard and lock-frame.
Second—Loosen the screw that fastens the mainspring to the trigger-guard, and turn the spring from under the tumbler of the hammer.
Third—Remove the trigger-guard, by turning out the three screws that fasten it to the lock-frame.
Fourth—Turn out the screw, and remove the double spring that bears upon the trigger and bolt.
Fifth—Turn out the screw-pins that hold the trigger and bolt in their places.
Sixth—Turn out the remaining side screw-pin, and remove the hammer with hand attached, by drawing it downwards out of the lock-frame. Clean all the parts and oil them thoroughly.

TO PUT THEM TOGETHER.

Replace the hammer with hand attached, then the bolt, the trigger, the trigger-guard, the mainspring, and finally the handle; returning each of the screws in their proper places, the arm is again fit for use.

☞ The Arms can be obtained, Wholesale and Retail, of the Manufacturer and Patentee,

SAMUEL COLT, 1, SPRING GARDENS, COCKSPUR STREET, LONDON

Or through any respectable Gun Dealer, Mercantile House, Army and Navy or E. I. Agent.

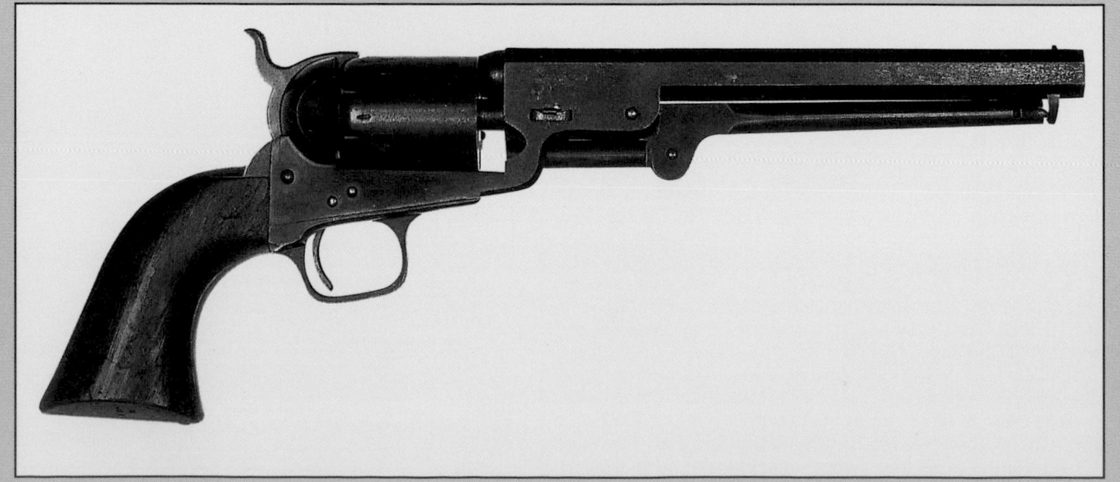

These pages, top to bottom: **An ornate Old Model Navy Pistol, (such pistols were given as gifts to influential people); an engraved New Model Pocket Pistol 'sidehammer Colt,' circa 1855; and a London Colt.**

Charles Dickens Tours Colt's Ill-Fated London Factory (1855)

We are on the threshold of Colonel Colt's factory in the somber and smoky region of Millbank. Under the roof of this low, brickbuilt, barrack-looking building, we are told that we may see what cannot be seen under one roof elsewhere in all England, the complete manufacture of a pistol, from dirty pieces of timber and rough bars of cast steel, till it is fit for the gunsmith's case. To see the same thing in Birmingham and in other places where firearms are made almost entirely by hand labour, we should have to walk about a whole day, visiting many shops carrying on distinct branches of the manufacture; not to speak of the toolmakers, the little screw and pin makers; all of whose work is done here. 'We are independent people,' says my informant, 'and are indebted to no one, save the engine and fixed machine makers.' This little pistol which is just put into my hand will pick into more than 200 parts, every one of which parts is made by a machine. A little skill is required in polishing the wood, in making cases, and in guiding the machines; but mere strength of muscle, which is so valuable in new societies, would find no market here, for the steam engine—indefatigably toiling in the hot, suffocating smell of rank oil, down in the little stone chamber below—performs nine-tenths of all the work that is done here. Neat, delicate-handed little girls do the work that brawny smiths still do in other gunshops. Most of them have been seamstresses and dressmakers, unused to factory work, but have been induced to conquer some little prejudice against it, by the attraction of better pay than they could hope to get by needlework. Even the men have, with scarcely an exception, been hitherto ignorant of gunmaking. No recruiting sergeant ever brought a more miscellaneous group into the barrack-yard, to be drilled more rapidly to the same duty, than these 200 hands have been. Carpenters, cabinet-makers, ex-policemen, butchers, cabmen, hatters, gas-fitters, porters—or at least one representative from each of those trades—are steadily drilling and poring at lathes all day in upper rooms.

The girls here earn from two to three shillings per day; the boys the same. The men get from three to eight shillings per day of 10 hours; while one or two, being quick, clever and reliable, are paid regularly 12 shillings per day. What is commonly called piecework is not the system usually adopted here. It has been found to tempt the men to hurry their work at the expense of a neat finish, and the manager prefers to give a workman six months trial, during which he learns the business of gunmaking by machinery, and he is also sure by that time to have shown what wages he is worth. Only 12 of these people are Americans; one or two Germans, the rest English.

Above: **Charles Dickens—perhaps pondering Colt's unique London factory, whose mass-production techniques were much different than any manufacturing process with which English gunsmiths were acquainted.**

Listening to these facts as my conductor communicates them, we pass into a long room hung with portraits of targets as they appeared after firing at them with Colt's revolvers. All the bullet marks are, of course, very near the bull's eye—which, I hope I am not presumptuous or depreciatory of the great Colt invention in attributing in some measure to the marksman. Beyond this is the storeroom, lined with wooden racks up to the ceiling, which are almost naked now, only five pistols of all the number that are made here—600 a week—being at the moment in store.

Out of the hot atmosphere, and the all-pervading odor of hot oil, we pass a yard ankle deep in iron chips (which make a dry hard road in all weathers, very destructive to leather) into a long outbuilding in which the only genuine smiths are at work. Here the very beginning of the pistols is made—if we except the cutting and polishing of the stock, which have been already described in these pages. There is little of the noise of a smithy here, except the roaring of the furnaces. A workman rams the end of a long bar of steel into the fire, and taking it out glowing with heat, strikes a bit off the end as if it were a stick of peppermint, while his companion—giving it a couple of rough taps upon the anvil—drops the red hot morsel into a die. This die is a plug hole, shaped something like a horseshoe, at the foot of a machine bearing a painful resemblance to a guillotine. While they have been breaking off the bit of steel, a huge screw has been slowly lifting up the iron hammerhead, which plays the part of the axe in the guillotine; and now the great hammer drops, and with one stroke beats the piece of iron to the form of the die. It has cooled to a black heat now, and is shaped something like the sole of a narrow shoe; but it must be heated again and the heel end beat up at right angles to the long part—taking care that it is bent according to the grain of the metal, without which it will be liable to flaw. Thus the shield, and what may be called the body of the pistol, are made in an instant.

In Birmingham, the barrels of firearms are made of old nails that have been knocked about, and which are melted, rolled into sheets, twisted again, and beaten about till they are considered to be tougher and less likely to burst—but the American gunsmiths know nothing about this. They merely beat it with steam hammers; for it would not do to draw it through holes, as thick wire is drawn, or to roll it as with ordinary round bars. These hammers are fixed, five in a frame, where they quiver with a chopping noise too rapidly to count the strokes, over a little iron plate, never touching it, though coming very close. Into the first of these the smith thrusts the red end of the bar, and guides it till it is beaten square. The next hammer beats it smaller, but still square. The next beats it smaller and longer still, but rounder. The fourth hammer beats it round, and the fifth strikes off the exact length for the barrel. This gradual process is absolutely necessary, for the steel will not bear being beaten round the first time; and, although five barrels may be thus forged in one minute, the rapid strokes of these hammers are said to make it quite as tough as the Birmingham plan; which seems to be borne out by the results at the proof-house. On the same floor, the barrels and cylinders, after polishing, are casehardened and tinted blue by burning in hot embers—processes which are well known.

Across the yard strewn with chips of iron again, and through the tool room, where men are turning great screws and other bolts and portions of machinery, we mount to the first floor and enter a long room filled with machines, and rather more redolent of hot rank oil. Considering that the floor supports a long vista of machinery in full action, the place looks clean and neat, and is not very noisy. Girls quietly attending to the boring and rifling of the barrels—having nothing to do but to watch the lathe narrowly, and drop a little oil upon the borer with a feather now and then—men drilling cylinders, holding locks to steam files, cutting triggers, slotting screws, treating cold iron everywhere as if it were soft wood, to be cut to any shape, without straining a muscle. It would be difficult and tedious to describe these machines minutely, although they are very interesting to a spectator, and cannot, I believe, be seen elsewhere. Every one of them is a simple lathe; but it is in the various cutters, borers and riflers that the novelty and ingenuity exist. Where the thing is to be made of eccentric shape, the cutter is of eccentric shape also; and although the superintendent of each machine acquires more or less skill by practice, it is in the perfection of these cutters and borers that the guarantee for uniformity consists. The bores of barrels and cylinders must be mathematically straight, and every one of the many parts must be exactly a duplicate of another. No one part belongs, as a matter of course, to any other part of one pistol; but each piece may be taken at random from a heap, and fixed to and with the other pieces until a complete weapon is formed, that weapon being individualized by a number stamped upon many of its component parts. The advantage of these contrivances is obvious. In every case of revolvers are placed, when sold, a number of such parts of a pistol as are most liable to accident; and with these, any soldier or sailor may, in a few minutes, repair his own weapon.

All this time we have been seeing only the making of little bits of a pistol. Pausing for a moment to see the engraving of a ship in full sail, and other ornamental work—including the maker's name stamped by great pressure on the cylinder—we come into a great room, where all the minute portions are brought to be examined. Here, by means of gauges, but chiefly by the practised eye of the superintendent, each separate article is examined, and rejected if in the slightest degree faulty. From this room the various parts are served out to the workmen who put them together and turn out the complete revolver.

Here is the proving room, where the pistols undergo a preparatory trial, before being sent up for the regular government proof. It is by no means the dark, mysterious iron-plated room in which I have been taught to believe that guns are proved, but an ordinary workshop, with two square wooden pipes, fixed horizontally, and open at the end, breast high. I am invited to prove a pistol, by firing it into one of these pipes which, I am told, afford sufficient protection to the firer in case of a barrel bursting—an event, pains were taken to assure me, of very rare occurrence. After a little practice, I find that a mere novice may, with one hand, discharge the six rounds as rapidly as the eye can wink.

—Charles Dickens
Household Words (Chapter 15, Volume 9)

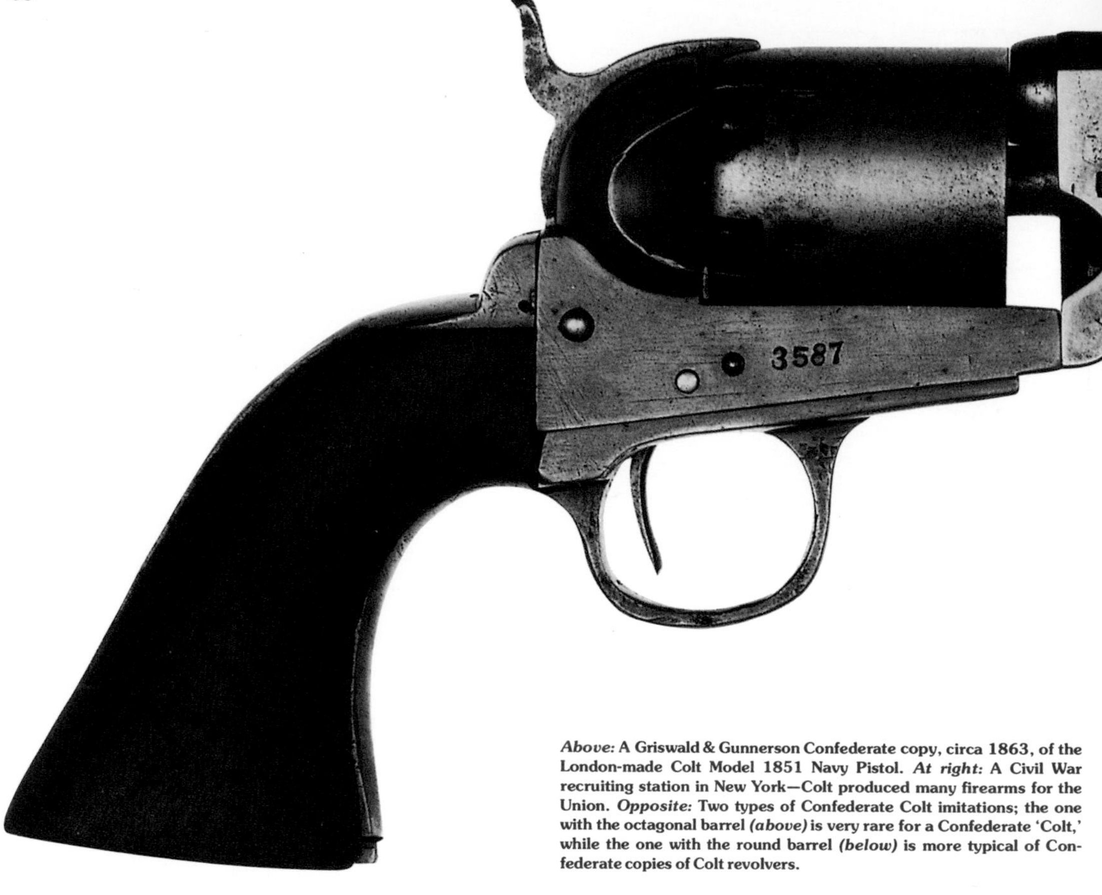

Above: **A Griswald & Gunnerson Confederate copy, circa 1863, of the London-made Colt Model 1851 Navy Pistol.** ***At right:*** **A Civil War recruiting station in New York—Colt produced many firearms for the Union.** ***Opposite:*** **Two types of Confederate Colt imitations; the one with the octagonal barrel** ***(above)*** **is very rare for a Confederate 'Colt,' while the one with the round barrel** ***(below)*** **is more typical of Confederate copies of Colt revolvers.**

In 1854, the British government contracted with Colt to produce both large orders of revolvers and of the machinery for the manufacture of muskets.

Colt's genius was not confined merely to inventiveness and public relations. He was an organizer and a manager of the highest grade. He recognized almost from the beginning that in the production of a firearm, some pieces of the gun require more skill to produce than others. Obviously, if the fabrication of one firearm is assigned to one individual, that individual will have to be paid according to the most skilled labor required for those particular parts composing the gun. This was unfair, both to Colt and the employee, as well as the customer. The work, therefore, was divided into various divisions depending on the precision or skill required to produce the individual parts. Pay was graduated according to each worker at the skill level at which he functioned. A system of subcontracting was employed whereby the less skilled workman ran the basic machines and did the routine work while the more skilled men did the actual assembling of the arms and their final finishing.

Because all of the parts of a particular model of gun had to be interchangeable with other specimens of that same model, precision was of the utmost importance. This need led Colt to institute the standardization of gauges used in calibrating the machinery upon which the parts were produced. This meant that, standardization being assured, workmen were able to be paid according to their ability to produce. Henry Ford is traditionally credited with this kind of assembly line process, but it was Colt who had the basic concepts in mind—and in operation—long before Ford came onto the American scene. Only 10 percent of the cost of a given weapon was generally taken up with the wages of the men who ran the machines. Thus, Colt's profitably increased, yet he was able to sell his 'perfect' weapons at a very reasonable price.

All of these mass production techniques and the ideas and attitudes behind them were purely of American vintage. The British employees of Colt's factory in London could never seem to adjust themselves to such processes. Consequently, the London branch of Colt's factory closed in 1857. It was bought by others who attempted to produce Colt's pistols, but if Colt could not make the factory run, no one could. In a short time, the London Pistol Company ceased to exist.

But if Colt's English venture had not proven to be so profitable, his foresight and insight into the political instability of the US did. Colt sensed that because of the slavery issue and other economic factors, the North and the South would almost inevitably go to war. That conflict, he knew, would test the very existence of the Union itself. Being a Connecticut Yankee by birth and owing his success

to the American enterprise in general, Colt undertook to have his Hartford Factory work literally night and day to produce for the US Government in advance of the anticipated hostilities. He wrote to Mr Root, his general manager, to get '5000 or 10,000 ahead of each kind of firearm in production.' He wanted his people to 'make hay while the sun shines.' This they were able to accomplish by working double shifts. And since supply lines were—at this point in time—still undisturbed, the flow of raw materials for the arms were still easily accessible. Thus, when hostilities broke out, Colt was able to supply the government with its immediate and long range needs. By 1862, the Colt plant was, indeed, 'making hay while the sun shines.'

However, the frenzied pace of production had taken its toll on Samuel Colt. He had suffered a personal blow when one of his daughters died and this, combined with his desire to furnish the Union troops with all of the weapons that they needed, led him into a condition of nervous exhaustion. On

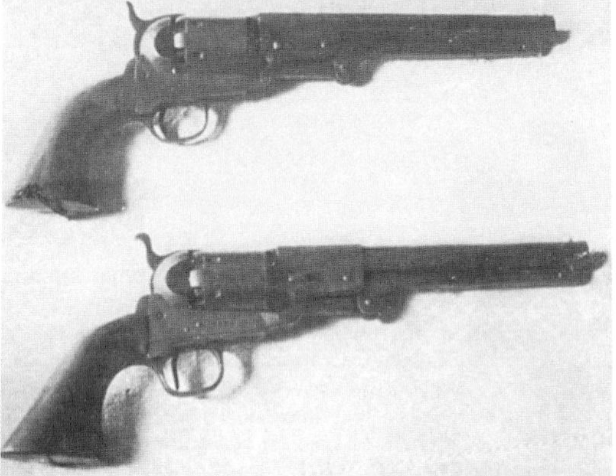

At top: **Colt's Hartford plant after the fire of 1864. Confederate spies in the plant were suspected of arson.** ***Above:*** **Back in the swing of things—the Colt factory as it looked after the rebuilding of the burned factory—1874. See also the pre-fire factory photo on page 21.**

his death bed, he was making plans to increase the size and output of the Hartford Factory by two-fold. He even contracted with the government to furnish 75,000 single shot muskets in addition to the revolver orders already filed with him. Colonel Samuel Colt died on 10 January 1862, being only 48 years of age.

His estate consisted of over 100 acres of prime land in Hartford, the largest private armory in the world and a corporation with paid up capital of over $1,000,000. The total value of his estate was estimated at $5,000,000. All of this is the more amazing when one considers that these accomplishments were done in a 14 year period. Not only had Samuel Colt, during this time, supplied his nation with the kinds of weapons that it needed and in sufficient quantities and made for himself a fortune; he had also established a standard of employee welfare that, even by today's standards, would be considered phenomenal. Colt's employees

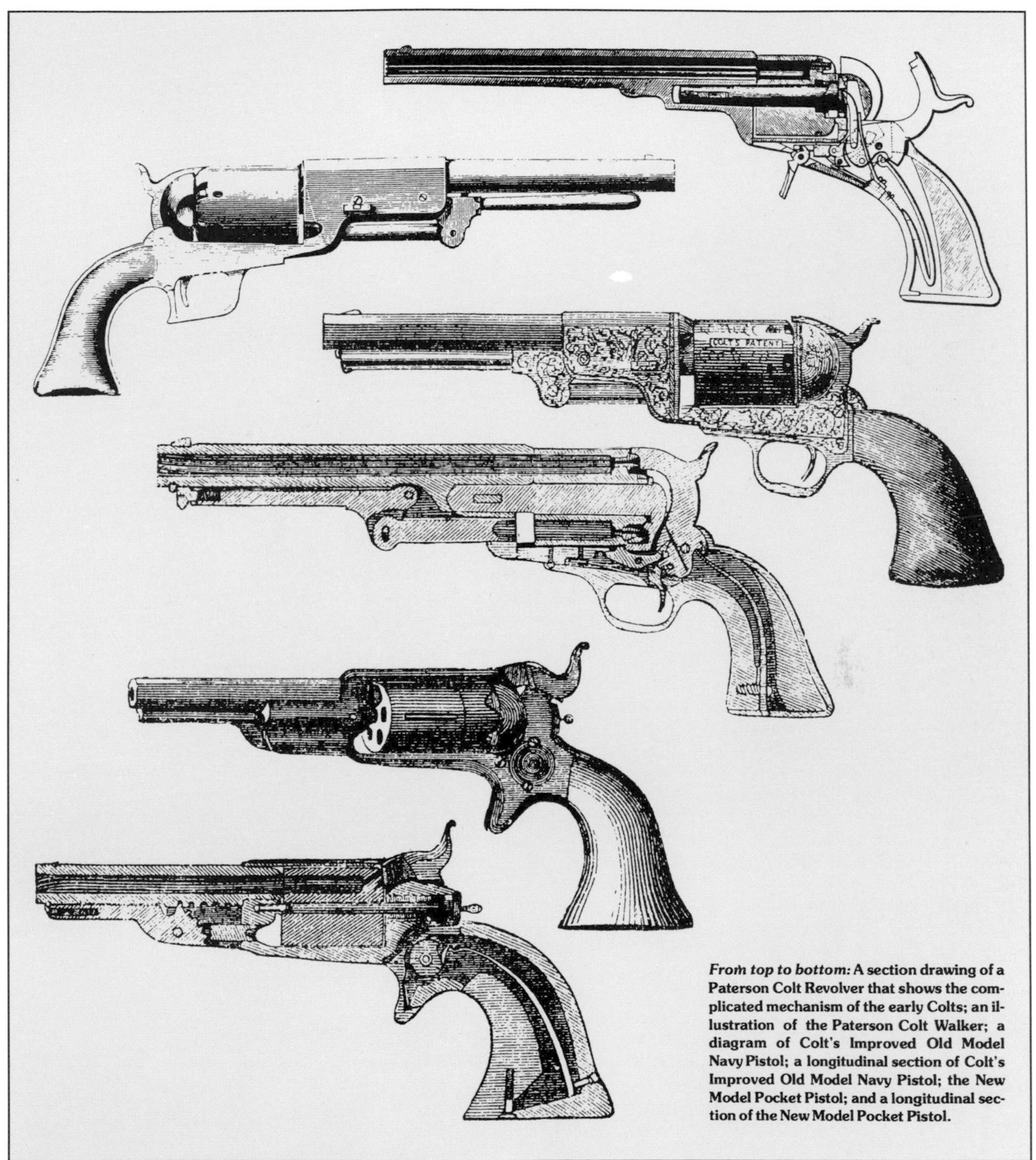

From top to bottom: **A section drawing of a Paterson Colt Revolver that shows the complicated mechanism of the early Colts; an illustration of the Paterson Colt Walker; a diagram of Colt's Improved Old Model Navy Pistol; a longitudinal section of Colt's Improved Old Model Navy Pistol; the New Model Pocket Pistol; and a longitudinal section of the New Model Pocket Pistol.**

worked in heated, well-lit, ventilated rooms with running water and at the highest pay in the country for the class of work that they did. They were even provided with up-to-date homes and a recreation center for their off hours. As a result, their loyalty to him personally and to the company, was unbounded. EK Root was elected the president upon Mr Colt's death.

The last models of Colt revolvers which were introduced before Mr Colt's death were the 1860 Army, the 1861 Navy and the 1862 Police and Pocket Navy. In February 1864, fire swept the old armory of the Hartford plant. The precision machines and floors of the plant had been saturated with nearly 10 years of accumulated oil. Eyewitness accounts attest to the ferocity of the blaze. Historians have speculated about the cause of the fire and most attribute it to Confederate spies in the plant itself. The total loss was nearly three quarters of a million dollars which was partly covered by insurance. It is interesting to note that during Colt's lifetime he carried no insurance, but had never had to worry very much about arson. Luckily, the fire did not occur until near the very end of the Civil War and the plant's destruction did not affect the outcome of the conflict.

A Tour of Colt's Hartford Factory (1857)

Leaving the office we cross the bridge, pass down through the machine shop, engine room, etc, to the rear parallel, an apartment 40 by 50 feet square, the center of which is appropriated as the storeroom for iron and steel. Large quantities of these materials, in bars and rods, are stored here in charge of a responsible party, whose duty it is to fill the orders from the contractors, and render an accurate statement of such deliveries to the main storekeeper's department. This latter system is universal throughout the establishment—thus, materials of all kinds can be readily accounted for, no matter what their state of transposition.

At this point it is well to inform the reader that almost the entire manual labor of the establishment is performed by contract. The contractors are furnished room, power, tools, material, heat, light—in fact all but muscle and brains; themselves, however, and their subordinates are all subject to the immediate government, as prescribed by the code of rules, laid down by the Company. The contractors number some scores—some particular manipulators requiring only their individual exertions, while others employ one to 40 assistants. Many of them are men of more than ordinary ability, and some have rendered themselves pecuniarily comfortable by their exertions.

We now pass into the forge shop, an apartment 40 by 200 feet square, comprising the whole of one arm of the parallel. Along each side range stacks of double-covered forges—the blasts for which, entering and discharging through flues in the walls, carry off the smoke and gases. Here, for the first time in our life, we were in a blacksmith shop in full operation, yet free from smoke and cinders, and with a pure atmosphere. Several kinds of hammers are used—those most in use, however, being 'drops' of the novel construction peculiar to the establishment; they are raised on the endless screw principle, and tripped by a trigger at the will of the operator. All the parts of the firearm composed of iron or steel are forged in swages, in which, although they may have ever so many preliminary operations, the shape is finally completed at a single blow. That some idea may be formed of the amount of work on a single rifle or pistol, we have determined to state the number of separate operations of each portion, and in each department. We adopt the 'Navy' or belt pistol, the weight of which is 38 ounces, as the example. In forging, the number of separate heats are enumerated: lockframe, two; barrel, three; lever, two; rammer, one; hammer two; hand, two; trigger, two; bolt, two; main spring, two; key, two; nipples, two each, 12; thus we find that no less than 32 separate and distinct operations, some of which contain in themselves several subdivisions, are required in the forging for a single pistol.

It is unnecessary to describe all the operations performed by the machines; a few will render the whole understandable. In all there are 36 separate operations before the cylinder is ready to follow the lockframe to the inspector. The barrel goes through 45 separate opera-

Touring Colt's Hartford factory—*opposite, left and right:* The Forging Shop and the Wareroom. *Above:* The dome-topped armory. This was no sweatshop—in fact, employees enjoyed unrivalled good working conditions for that era.

tions on the machines. The other parts are subject to about the following number: Lever, 27; rammer, 19; hammer, 28; hand, 20; trigger, 21; bolt, 21; key, 18; sear spring, 12; 14 screws, seven each, 98; six cones, eight each, 48; guard, 18; handlestrap, five ; and stock, five. Thus it will be observed that the greater part of the labor is completed in this department. Even all the various parts of the lock are made by machinery, each having its relative initial point to work from, and on the correctness of which the perfection depends.

As soon as completed the different parts are carried to the story above, which, with the exception of machinery and columns through the center, is an exact counterpart of the room below. It is designated the Inspecting and Assembling Department. Here the different parts are most minutely inspected; this embraces a series of operations which in the aggregate amount to considerable work; the tools to inspect a cylinder, for example, are fifteen in number, each of which must gauge to a hair. The greatest nicety is observed, and it is absolutely impossible to get a slighted piece of work beyond this point. On finishing his examination, the inspector punches his initial letter on the piece inspected, thus pledging his reputation on its quality.

The mountings, consisting of the handlestrap and guard, which are composed of gunmetal, are cast and afterward worked up in the machines in the same manner as the other metal work. The woodwork of the stock is also shaped by machinery.

Each part having been thus far completed in itself, now comes the first uniting or 'assembling,' as the workmen term it. Let us get our Navy pistol in shape; to do so we will want a cylinder, barrel, lockframe, hammer, trigger, bolt, key, mainspring, hand, sear spring, lever, rammer, guard, back strap, stock and a number of peculiar screws. These are readily united by the assembler, and our pistol assumes its material shape, It is now numbered; to make it special, we will designate our number as 138,565; the imprint of the establishment, 'Address Colonel Sam Colt, Hartford, Conn' is also stamped on at this time. It is now carefully taken apart, all the pieces being stamped the particular number of the arm; and thus our barrel, cylinder and etc, each with a quantity of his fellows, are taken away for their final finishing.

Most of the metal work is carried to the dry polishing shop—a room 60 feet square, located in the third story of the center building. Here it is polished on emery and other wheels, about half a yard in diameter, the operatives sitting at their work. After inspection, the barrels and cylinders are handed over for the blueing process—an operation that requires nicety and practical experience. The ovens for this, as well as for the casehardening—to which process all the iron work is submitted—as well as the forges for tempering the springs, etc, are located in the forge shop. From the polishers, the mountings go to the electroplaters—who occupy a room 25 by 40, in the basement of the office building, where they are plated with silver, and afterward burnished. The woodwork returns to the stock maker's shop—a room 60 by 80, in the third story of the center building. This is supplied with power saws, planes, morticing and shaping machines and as throughout the whole establishment, every means is

adopted for labor saving. The stock then comes back for varnishing and the final finishing.

On their final completion, all the parts are delivered to the general storekeeper's department, a room 60 feet wide by 190 feet long, situated in the second story of the central building, and extending over the rear parallel, All the hand tools and materials (except the more bulky kinds) are distributed to the workmen from this place; several clerks are required to parcel the goods out and keep the accounts; in fact, it is a store, in the largest sense of the term, and rather on the wholesale principle at that. On the reception of finished, full sets of the parts of the pistols, they are once more carried up to the assembling room; but this time to another corps of artisans. Guided by the numbers, they are once more assembled; and now, although each portion has associated with scores of its fellows and gone through many distinct operations in distant parts of the establishment, our particular pistol, number 138,565, is reassembled as first united, and the finished firearm is laid on a rack, ready for the prover; of course many others accompany it to the department of this official, which is located in the third story of the rear building. Here each chamber is loaded with the largest charge possible, and practically tested by firing—after which they are cleaned out by the prover and returned to the inspection department. The inspectors again take them apart, thoroughly clean and oil them; then they are for the last time put together and placed in a rack for the final inspection. The parts having been so thoroughly examined and tested, it would seem that this last inspection was scarcely necessary; but, after a short observation, we saw several laid aside. Taking up one with a small mark on the barrel, 'Why do you reject this?' we inquired. 'Pass that today, and probably much larger blemishes would appear tomorrow,' replied Mr T. The order from the Principal is perfection; and a small scratch in the blueing or varnish is sufficient to prevent the arm passing. The finished arm finally passing the inspection, is now returned to the storeroom—from whence, after being papered, they are sent to the wareroom, situated in the basement of the office building; from this they are sent to nearly every portion of the habitable globe.

Besides the great degree of uniformity and precision arrived at by the adaption of machinery in this manufacture, which exactness could be compassed in no other manner, it is stated that a number sufficient to supply the present demand could not be produced by manual labor alone. During the time of our visit we were informed that scarcely less than 100,000 weapons were at that moment in the various stages of progress, yet the whole number of employees was a little less than 600 who, by the aid of mechanical contrivances, turn out an average of 250 finished arms per diem.

In round numbers it might be stated that supposing the cost of an arm to be $100; of this the wages of those who attended to and passed the pieces through the machines was 10 percent, and those of the best class workmen engaged in assembling or putting together, finishing and ornamenting the weapons was also 10 percent, thus leaving 80 percent for the duty done by the machinery.

With the exception of the steam engine and boilers, a majority of the machinery was not only invented, but constructed on the premises. When this department was commenced, it was the intention of the company to manufacture solely for their own use. Some months since, applications were made by several foreign governments to be supplied with machines and the right to operate them. After mature deliberation, it was concluded to supply orders, and on the day of our visit we saw a complete set of machinery, for manufacturing firearms, that will shortly be shipped to a distant land. The company has now determined to incorporate this manufacture as a branch of their regular business.

Employees' Welfare

Although so much care and attention have been exercised in perfecting the armory and its accessories and products, the general welfare of the employees has not been neglected; extensive arrangements for their comfort and convenience are in the course of rapid completion.

And we may here remark that they are deserving of such especial favor; as a body they are mostly young men, many of them having commenced their business life in the establishment. It was, in a measure, necessary to educate men expressly for the purpose, as the manipulation required is not exclusively that of the gunsmith, or of the machinist, but a combination of both of these callings. Taken as a whole, we found them decidedly a reading and thinking community, and we venture the assertion that it would be difficult to produce a counterpart of their mental capacity in the same number of mechanics employed in a manufactory. That they are well compensated for their services is evident from the fact of the payroll amounting to from $1000 to $1200 per day.

The grounds around the armory have been laid out in squares of 500 feet each by streets 60 feet wide; upon these squares are being erected commodious three-story dwellings. Sufficient for about 80 families have already been finished, and are occupied by the employees; the operations will be continued until all who desire are accommodated. These houses have all the conveniences of city life. Gasworks, of sufficient capacity to supply as large a population as can occupy the area, have already been erected and put into operation.

One of the buildings is a beautiful structure known as Charter Oak Hall—so named from its being located on the same avenue as the venerable and time-honored tree, which for centuries braved the storm, and from a singular incident became celebrated in our colonial history. This hall is employed by the operatives for lectures, debates, concerts, balls and etc. The festive occasions are enlivened with music from a band organized from their midst—the instruments, which are most excellent, having been furnished through the liberality of Colonel Colt. A public park, fountains and etc, are in the plans, all of which are being successfully executed.

On the hill overlooking the whole is the palatial residence of the proprietor. It is really a superb edifice, the main building being 50 by 100 feet; it is in the Italian villa style—the ground and outbuildings being on the scale which would naturally be expected of a man of his extended views and liberal taste.

—*United States Magazine* (March 1857)

The tour continues—*clockwise from immediate left:* The Proving Room, the Dry Polishing Room, machinery for stocks and grips, and the main part of the armory—a room that was ranked as the best, most well-arranged and efficient workshop of its time.

Metallic

The history of self-exploding metallic cartridges actually began in France about 1812, with a Monsieur Pauly. The first types of this ammunition were actually made of paper which held the powder and the bullet, and only the rear of the cartridge was brass, with its depression to hold a detonator. When the cartridge was fired, the paper holding the powder and bullet were consumed in the explosion. In later improvements in cartridges of this kind, the paper shells were discarded in favor of a rolled cardboard—somewhat similar to our modern shotgun shells.

In 1847 Monsieur Haulier patented the idea of a self-contained cartridge that employed copper and brass in its construction. These types of shells were of very small caliber, and the first metallic cartridge to come to the United States (in the mid-1850s) was an early .22 short. Once arriving in America, the metallic cartridge soon took on more standard forms of construction, and was also being made in larger calibers.

Of course, these cartridges are the mainstay of the firearms industry today, and the four key elements of their original construction are the four elements common to all cartridges presently. The first of these elements is the case, which is made out of expandable metal, which, even though it expands upon detonation, immediately contracts in size slightly, to allow removal from the chamber. The second element is, of course, the explosive material, a gunpowder of some sort, which is loaded into the case. The third element is the bullet or projectile, which is crimped or fitted into the case in some manner. And the fourth element is the primer, or explosive device, which, when the hammer strikes it, detonates the powder.

When metallic cartridges were first introduced in the mid-1800s, the primer was generally of a fulminate of mercury compound. The explosive was generally black powder, which produced great amounts of smoke and flame, and bullets were generally of pure lead.

By the time of the Civil War, at least two repeating rifles, each employing metallic cartridges, were in use. They were the Henry rifle and the Spencer rifle. These two rifles were in .24 caliber and .56 caliber respectively.

It is interesting to note that the first metallic cartridges were of the 'folded head' type. Their distinguishing feature was that even though they were self contained, they could not be reloaded after they were fired. This proved to be quite a disadvantage, and naturally, other designs were brought forth, particularly by a Mr Bearden, who invented the 'boxer' type of center fire cartridge with a drawn brass case, which could be reloaded.

The ability of Bearden's case to withstand the blow of the hammer and retain its shape was of such tremendous advantage that Army regulations for many years called for soldiers to both save and reload their fired ammo cases.

The metallic cartridge revolution was actually first seen in rifles, not pistols. But it was not long before the idea took shape to use these new cartridges in revolving cylinder handguns. But a particular legal entanglement over a certain patent by Rollin White prevented the use of center fire cartridges in revolving pistols for some years. White had taken out a patent which involved the loading of shot and the recapping of primers from the rear of the cylinder. This concept was later adapted into a rimfire .22 caliber pistol. This particular pistol was never a commercial success, but

Cartridges

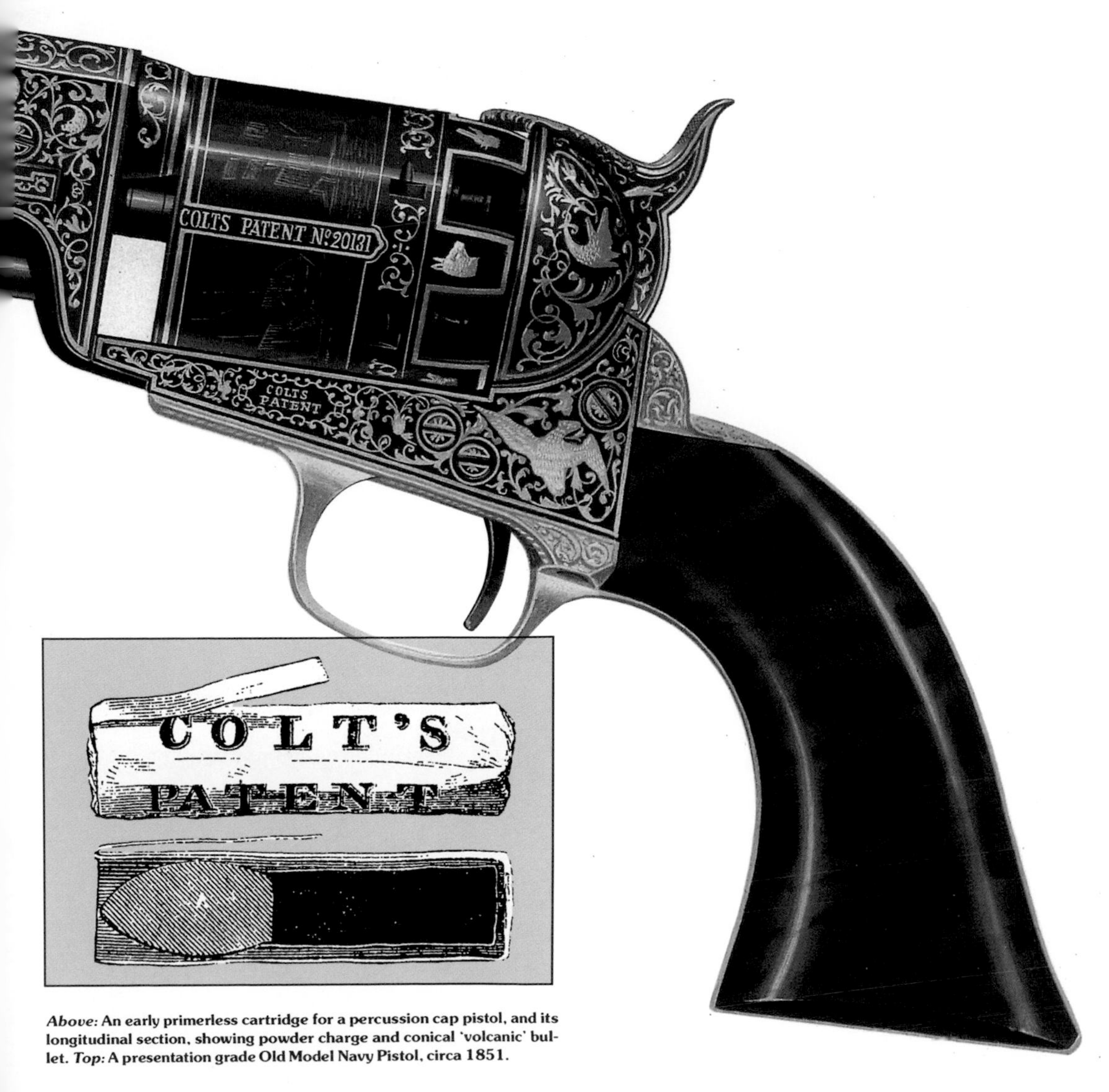

Above: An early primerless cartridge for a percussion cap pistol, and its longitudinal section, showing powder charge and conical 'volcanic' bullet. *Top:* A presentation grade Old Model Navy Pistol, circa 1851.

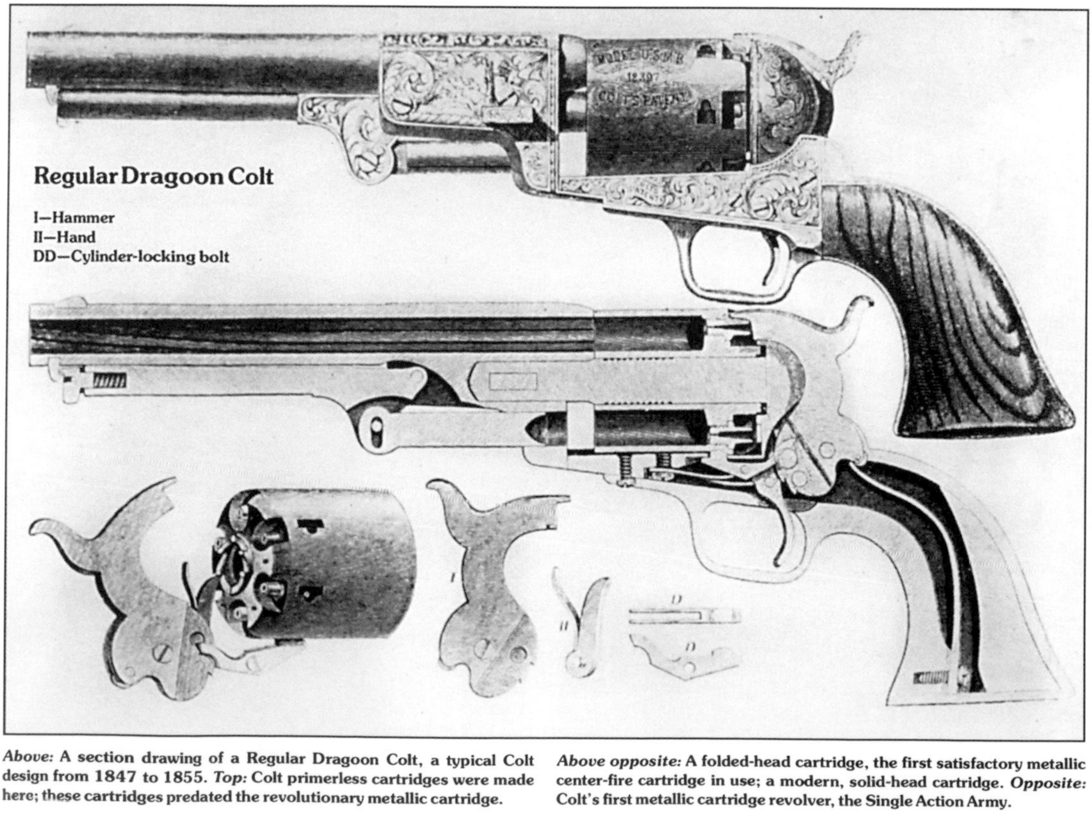

Regular Dragoon Colt

I—Hammer
II—Hand
DD—Cylinder-locking bolt

Above: A section drawing of a Regular Dragoon Colt, a typical Colt design from 1847 to 1855. *Top:* Colt primerless cartridges were made here; these cartridges predated the revolutionary metallic cartridge.

Above opposite: A folded-head cartridge, the first satisfactory metallic center-fire cartridge in use; a modern, solid-head cartridge. *Opposite:* Colt's first metallic cartridge revolver, the Single Action Army.

the ideas behind it were patented, and were therefore unavailable to other arms manufacturers—at least while the patent stood.

Another factor that prevented the quick conversion from cap and ball to cartridges was the fact that cartridges were not widely produced, and were therefore not readily available to the public. But the advantages of cartridges were overwhelming, and where there was a will, a way would be found. The great conversion from cap and ball to cartridges was underway. It would take many turns, but in the end cartridges would win out.

Because the cartridge revolution had first taken place in rifles and long arms, naturally, gun owners wanted to convert their cap and ball pistols to be able to use the same cartridges as their long arms. Since most of the long arms which used cartridges were of .44 caliber, it was natural that the first pistols were of .44 and .45 caliber, also.

Actually, the conversion of a cap and ball pistol into a cartridge pistol was relatively simple. The nipples, which held the caps in place, were simply cut away, leaving an open hole in the rear of the cylinder, large enough to accommodate the cartridge. The hammer was then modified such that when it was released, the primer at the rear of the cartridge was struck forcibly enough to set off the powder. Of course the rammer—which was indispensable for the loading of a cap and ball pistol—was no longer needed, and was usually removed as a part of the conversion process.

But centerfire cartridges were still hard to obtain, and so many folks of the time took to carrying two separate cylinders with them. One of the percussion cap type, and the other of the new cartridge type.

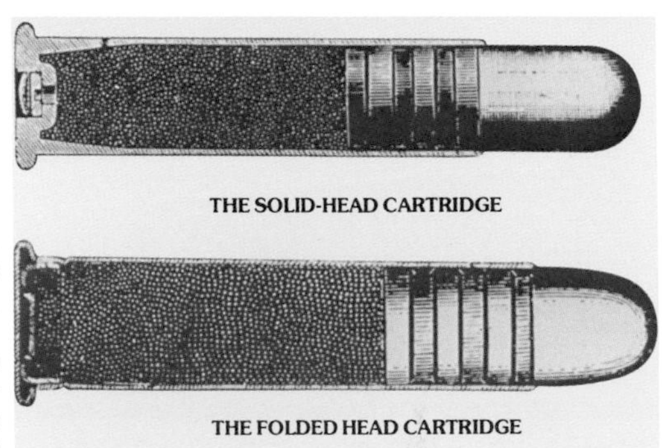

THE SOLID-HEAD CARTRIDGE

THE FOLDED HEAD CARTRIDGE

Later, another alteration of importance took place. This was Mr Thuer's patent which was taken out in 1868. It incorporated small firing pins in the cylinder itself—thus negating the need to alter the cap and ball hammer.

As can be seen from the above, this alteration process from cap and ball to cartridges was momentous enough to generate its own set of patents. The alteration process itself made money for the gunmakers as well. Colt accepted contracts with the government for alterations of all revolvers in the hands of all of the Armed Services of the United States Government in 1872.

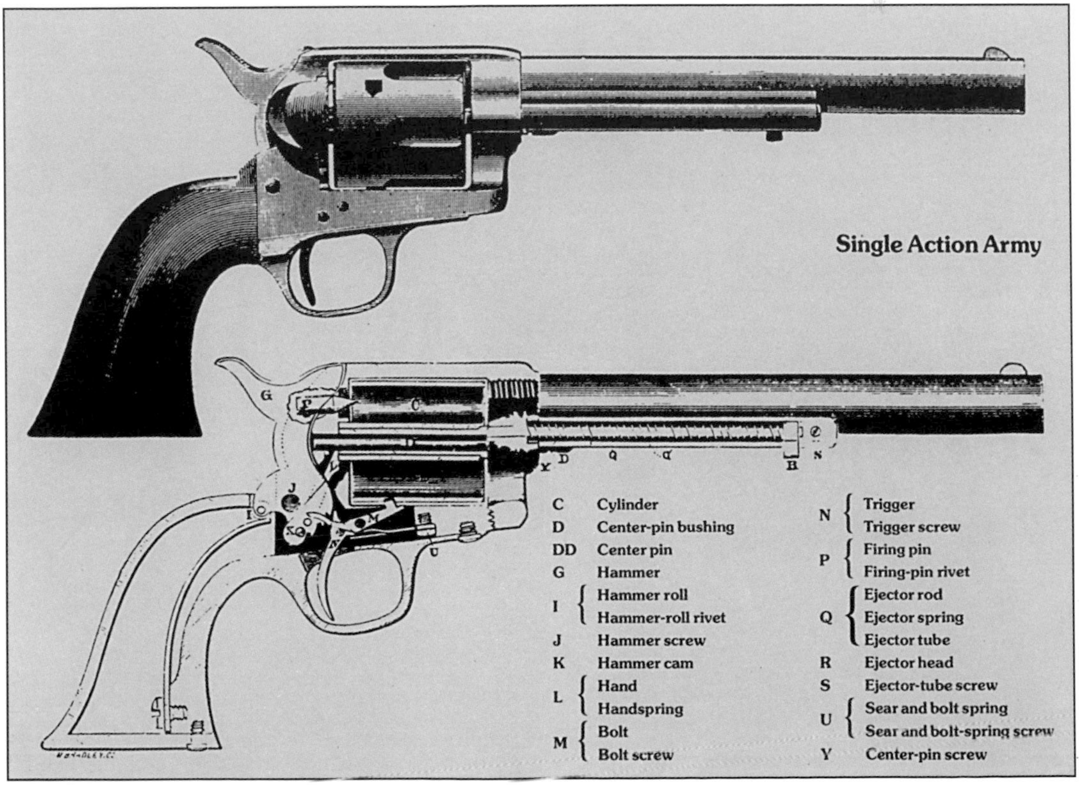

Single Action Army

- C Cylinder
- D Center-pin bushing
- DD Center pin
- G Hammer
- I Hammer roll; Hammer-roll rivet
- J Hammer screw
- K Hammer cam
- L Hand; Handspring
- M Bolt; Bolt screw
- N Trigger; Trigger screw
- P Firing pin; Firing-pin rivet
- Q Ejector rod; Ejector spring; Ejector tube
- R Ejector head
- S Ejector-tube screw
- U Sear and bolt spring; Sear and bolt-spring screw
- Y Center-pin screw

Great Colts Nineteenth

Above: An ornate example of the Colt Single Action Army Target Model, which is basically the same—aside from its 7.5 inch barrel—as the famous Colt 'Peacemaker' Frontier Model Single Action Army Revolver.

of the Century

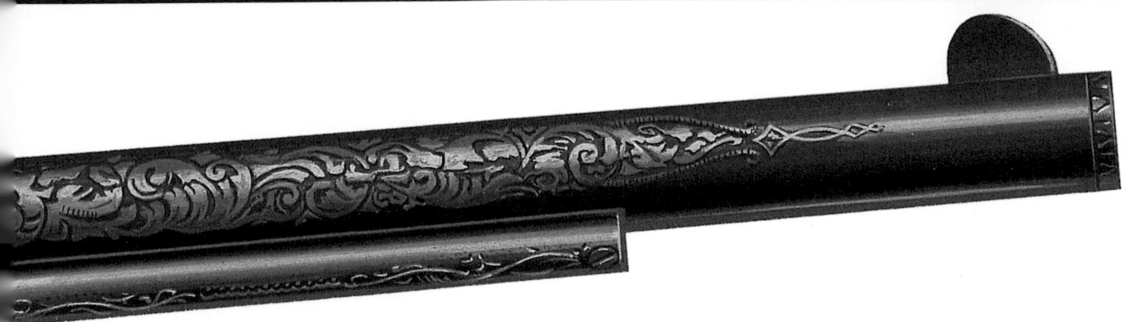

The 'Peacemaker,' The Gun that Won the West

The Peacemaker was the first cartridge pistol produced by the Colt Company. It was first officially known as the New Model Army Metallic Cartridge Revolving Pistol, and later renamed Single Action Army Revolver.

This weapon was a .45 caliber pistol using the new self-contained center-fire cartridges. Up to 40 grains of black powder could be packed behind its 235 grain lead bullet. But the government initially chose to pack only 28 grains of black powder instead of the maximum 40.

The Single Action Army Revolver was initially produced in 1871, and by 1873, the first order of 8000 was placed by the Army's Ordnance Department. There were basically three barrel lengths available for the Single Action Army Revolver, and these were representative of the three basic markets employing such a weapon. The Cavalry Model had a barrel length of 7.5 inches. This was to facilitate long-range accuracy. The standard or Artillery Model had a barrel length of 5.5 inches. And for civilians, a 4.75 inch barrel model was made available.

Since the availability of cartridges was somewhat limited on the frontiers, and since most customers carried both a sidearm as well as a rifle, the Single Action Army was quickly tooled to use .44-40 caliber ammunition, so as to match the caliber of the very popular 1873 Winchester Repeating Rifle. This was not simply a matter of convenience to frontiersmen. The ability to have both of one's firearms chambered for the same cartridge could mean the difference between life and death in certain situations.

There is a particular type of Single Action Army Pistol called the Buntline Special, which has caused some confusion among historians. The Buntline Special got its name, not from anyone at the Colt factory, but rather from a Ned Buntline, who was a prolific writer of the period. Buntline specialized in writing about the Wild West. On trips into the West, he presented various distinguished frontiersmen with Army Colts with 12-inch barrels and shoulder stocks. Wyatt Earp and Bat Masterson were among those to receive such weapons. It is doubtful, however, that there was much practically to pistols with foot-long barrels. They were mainly for gift and show purposes. Obviously, Buntline found it more sensational to write about characters shooting it out in the streets of the Wild West with pistols of extraordinary barrel length rather than more conventional arms.

The Single Action Army Pistol provided the overall pattern for 'six-shooter' type Colt pistols up to the present time. It is the gun that is the most easily recognized as being a Colt by the general public, and indeed its appearance is deeply etched into the American psyche. The Single Action Army became the Frontier Colt. It was the 'Peacemaker' that stood between the law abiding and the outlaws. Wild Bill Hickok and Wyatt Earp (the first marshall of Dodge City, then Wichita, Kansas—and finally Tombstone, Arizona), used their Colts to blaze their way into the history of the Wild West. And of course, desperados and anti-heros had them also. William Bonney, alias Billy the Kid, did his murderous work with Colts. Even the brash and wily General George Armstrong Custer vainly relied on his Single Action Armys when justice was done at the battle of the Little Big Horn.

Legend has it that the renown of the Old Frontier Six-Shooter was such that it was 'not God or the Declaration of Independence that made men free and equal, but, rather,

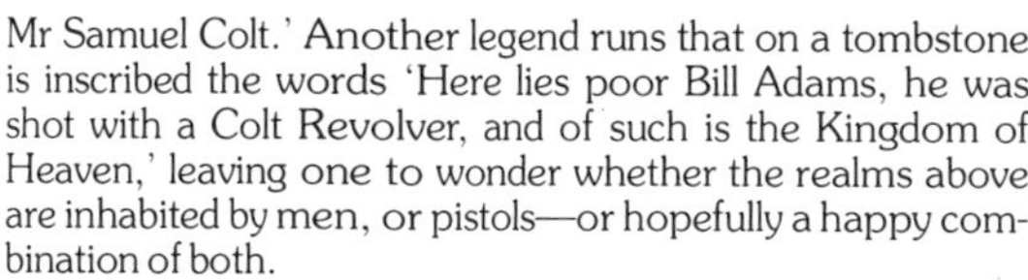

Left: **General George Custer was known for his pair of fancy Colts.** ***Above:*** **Early cowboy movie star William S Hart brandishes his Peacemakers.** ***Right:*** **Patent drawings for the Peacemaker show metallic cartridges in its chambers, and how its chambers align with its barrel.**

Mr Samuel Colt.' Another legend runs that on a tombstone is inscribed the words 'Here lies poor Bill Adams, he was shot with a Colt Revolver, and of such is the Kingdom of Heaven,' leaving one to wonder whether the realms above are inhabited by men, or pistols—or hopefully a happy combination of both.

When their lives depended on it, men and women depended on their Colt revolver. In the movie *The Shootist*, John Wayne explains to a young boy that to survive a gunfight is not so much a matter of speed and accuracy as it is a matter of being 'willing.' And when men had to rely upon their 'willingness,' they found their Colts to be equally as willing and reliable.

Other Great Revolvers

In the years after the Civil War, the nation was expanding westward, the South was rebuilding, and the overall tenor of the times was one of flux and change, expansion and competition. In this atmosphere, a greater and greater need arose for personal protection. The National Arms Company had begun to produce small, single shot Deringer Pistols in the early 1870s. The Colt Company bought out the National Arms Company, and in so doing, inherited the Deringer line of small handguns. While the general public's concept of a Deringer-type pistol is that the weapon is of small caliber, the original Deringers were actually of .41 caliber, and thus packed quite a punch.

The first center fire pistols to appear on the market were all of single action variety. This meant that the hammer had to be cocked, thus revolving the cylinder before the trigger could be pulled. In the later 1870s, Colt introduced its new Double Action Self-Cocking Center Fire Six-Shot Revolver. The revolving of the cylinder into place was no longer dependent on the cocking of the hammer, but was rather now a function of the pulling of the trigger. When the trigger was pulled, the cylinder would almost instantaneously roll into place, and the hammer would miraculously pull itself into a cocked position and immediately would snap forward, firing the cartridge. This meant that all six shots in the cylinder could be fired as rapidly as the trigger could be pulled. Here was advancement indeed! Colt referred to this first double action pistol as the Lightning Model.

However, this first double action revolver did not meet with as much success as might have been anticipated. The number of internal parts required to produce such lightning speed was greatly increased, thus contributing to the overall weight and complexity of the weapon. Many continued to use their far more simple single action 'Peacemakers.'

By the early 1900s, however, the transition from single action to double action weapons was almost complete. An interesting variation on the double action revolver took

W. MASON.

Revolving Fire-Arms.

No. 158,957. Patented Jan. 19, 1875.

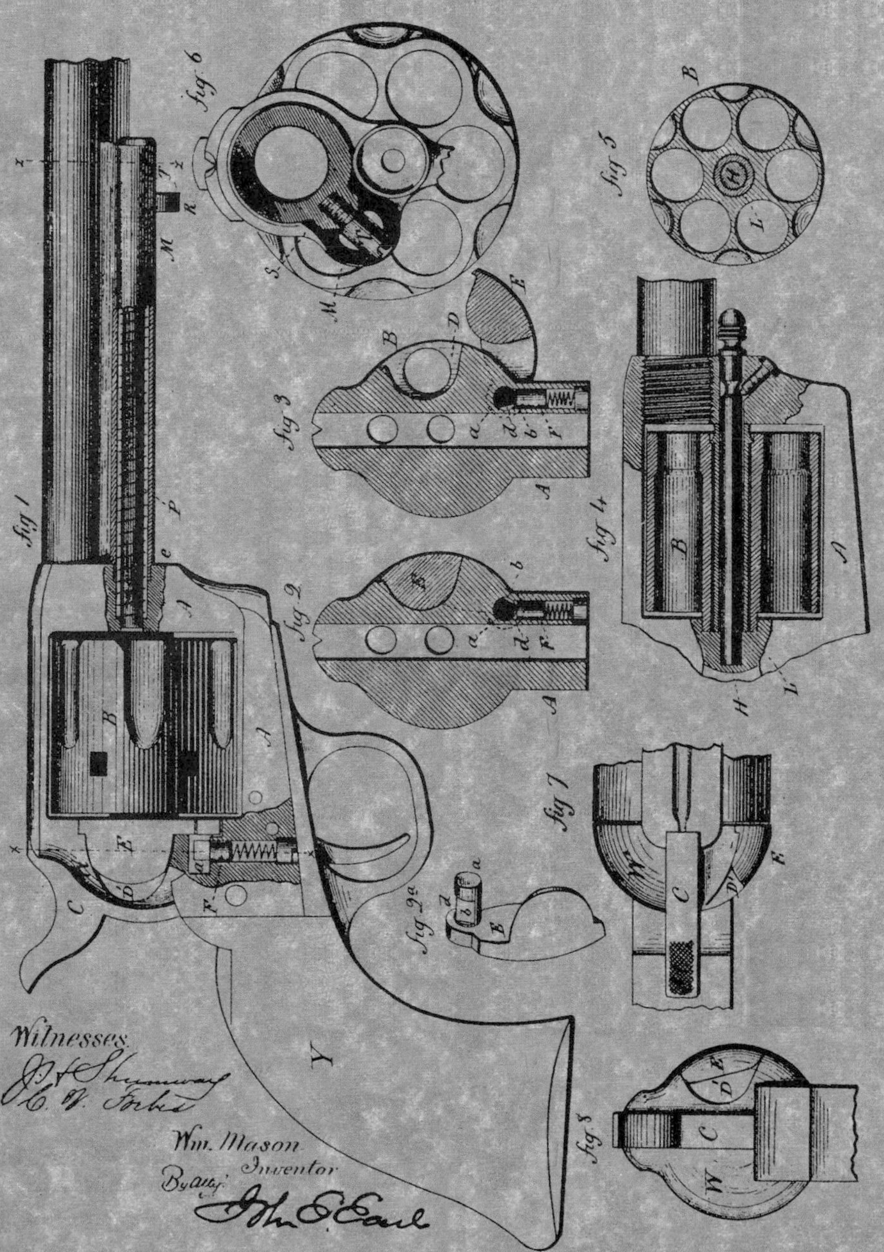

THE GRAPHIC CO. PHOTO-LITH 39 & 41 PARK PLACE N.Y.

Clockwise from immediate above: **A Double Action Army Model, circa 1877, with rounded mother-of-pearl grips; A Colt Number 1 Deringer, circa 1870; the Peacemaker repeatedly 'won the West' in Hollywood Westerns; Emmett Dalton, leader of the notorious Dalton Gang, owned this Single Action Frontier Model, which was used prior to the Coffeyville robbery in 1892.**

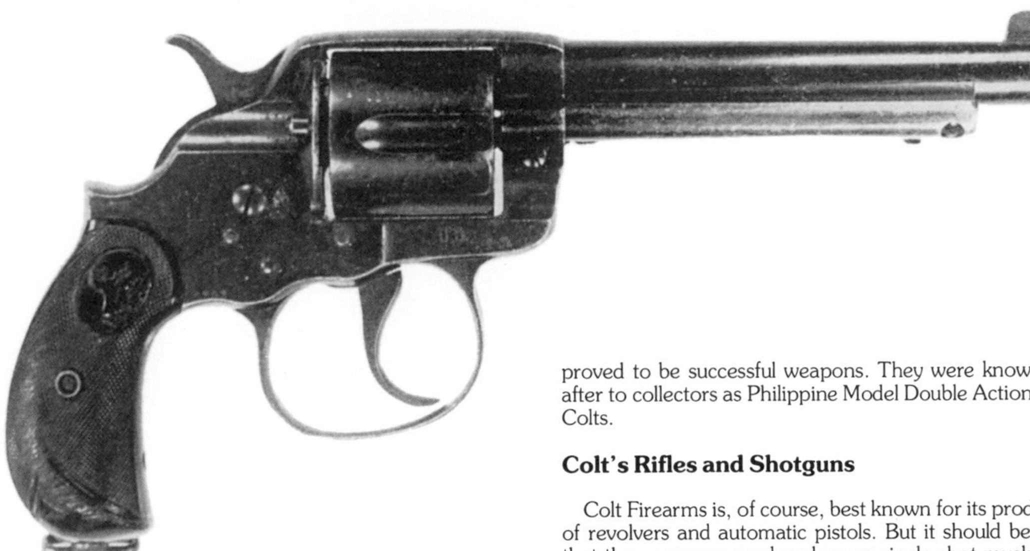

place in 1902. The government had contracted with Colt to produce some double action army models with wider triggers and enlarged trigger guards. Ostensibly, these weapons were to be used in Alaska, and the customized alterations were such that troops could more easily use the pistols in very severe weather where heavy gloves were required. These pistols originally bound for Alaska were of the .45 caliber variety. At the same time, American troops were engaging foes in the Philippine Islands, half a world away. The standard issue weapon in the Philippines at that time was .38 caliber Double Action Army Pistols. These were found, by experience, not to pack the firepower needed to successfully engage the enemies in deep jungle surroundings. So, in typical Army fashion, the Alaska-customized Colts were sent to the Philippines because of their larger caliber, and proved to be successful weapons. They were known ever after to collectors as Philippine Model Double Action Army Colts.

Colt's Rifles and Shotguns

Colt Firearms is, of course, best known for its production of revolvers and automatic pistols. But it should be noted that the company produced many single shot muskets for the Civil War, and between that time and the early 1900s, produced many different kinds of rifles and shotguns in both single and double-barreled varieties. A General Berdan of the US Army had patented a particular kind of bottlenecked center fire cartridge in the 1860s. The Colt Company built a rifle around this cartridge design known as the Berdan Russian Rifle. In 1870, the Russian Government contracted for the construction of 40,000 of these single shot, breech loading rifles.

In the later 1870s, Colt even produced both hammered and hammerless double-barreled shotguns, but both models were discontinued by 1900.

This business of placing two barrels side by side was, at first, thought to be a profitable idea. In about 1880, Colt produced a .45-70 double-barreled rifle. But the model soon fell into disfavor with the public and was discontinued, probably due to its excessive weight. Winchester had cap-

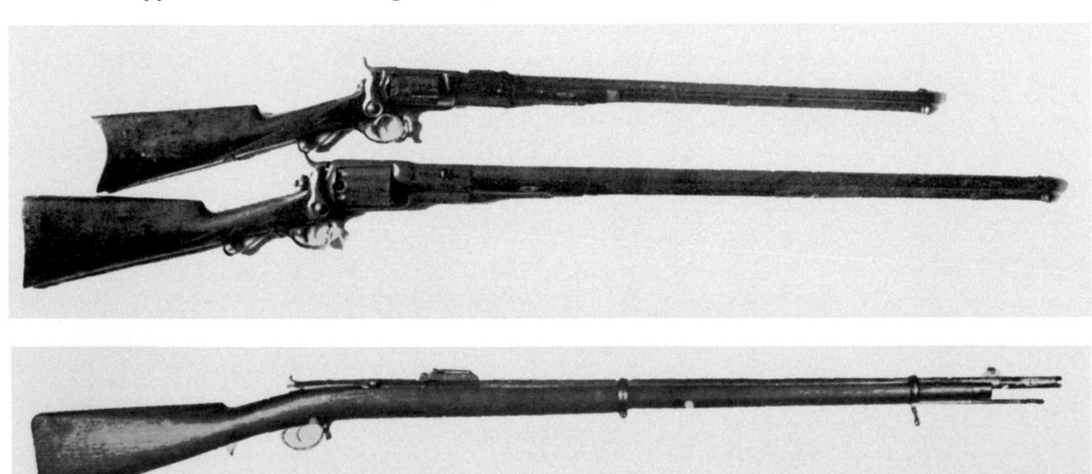

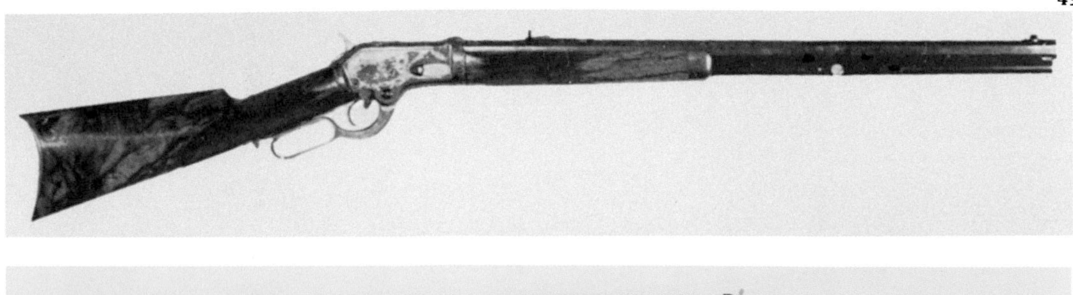

tured the market in rifles and carbines with their .44-40 caliber weapons. Colt attempted to capitalize on this popularity by bringing out, in 1883, the first Colt repeating rifle using the new cartridge ammunition. It was produced in both the shorter carbine size, as well as the longer rifle size, but only a little over 6000 specimens were produced.

In the mid-1880's, an altogether new type of repeating rifle appeared. It was known as the 'Lightning Magazine Rifle.' It was produced under a Dr Elliot's patents. It incorporated a 'trombone' action, which we know today to be the familiar 'pump' or 'slide action.' The old spent cartridge was ejected from the chamber, and a new one was mechanically inserted into place by the quick sliding action of the hand on a rail mounted parallel to the barrel. This allowed the user of the 'Colt Lightning Pump' to hold the rifle's trigger and work the slide, thus achieving a near-machine gun rate of fire. In some quarters, the Colt Lightning Pump is said to be 'the gun that *should have* won the West.'

But by the early 1900s, profitability was not to be found in the production of sporting arms, but, rather, in the manufacture of the new automatic pistols, rifles and mounted military weapons.

Clockwise from immediately above: **An early ad for Colt's Lightning Pumps; a Lightning Express .44–40 model; a Colt Berdan rifle for the Russian Army; Colt 1855 model revolving sidehammer shotgun (five shots) and rifle (six shots); Colt Phillipine model pistol; Colt's lever action 'Burgess' rifle; and Colt hammer and hammerless shotguns.**

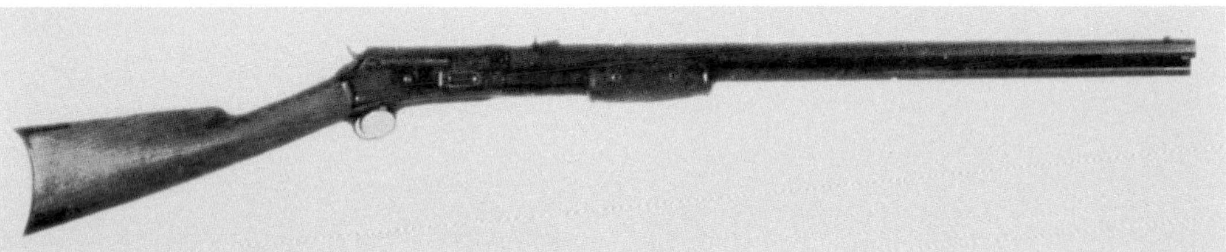

The Evolution Modern Colt

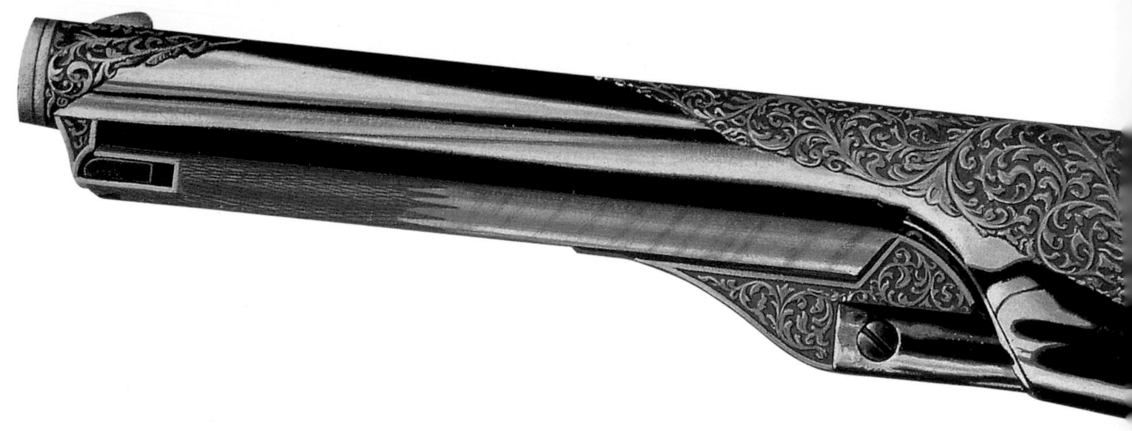

The modern era of Colt revolvers can actually be traced to the early 1890s, when Colt scored a resounding market victory over its competitors by introducing 'swingout' cylinders on its double-action revolvers. Prior to this time, many single and double-action revolvers had to be broken between the breech and the cylinder in order for the cartridges to be loaded. This placed the pistol in an inverted 'V' position in the user's hand. Alternately, many Colt revolvers had a 'reloading notch' offset at the rear of the cylinder. Shells were placed in their chambers by rotating the cylinder until an empty chamber aligned with the reloading notch, at which point the shell was manually loaded into the chamber. The rotating procedure was followed for unloading spent shells, with the exception that, at this point, the 'empties' were pushed out of their chambers with the famous offset ejector rod, which gave the Peacemaker its distinctive head-on appearance. But now the cylinder had only to be released from the overall frame and swung out on hinges in a sideways motion in order to facilitate unloading and loading. Colt was about 10 years ahead of its competitors at Smith and Wesson in this new innovation, and profited immensely by it.

The modern era of Colt Revolvers, at least, began with the Official Police Model, which went by the name of New Navy when it was first introduced in 1889. Variations on this basic model continued in subsequent years. The Pocket Positive, the Police Positive, and the New Service Revolvers are among the most famous of these early truly modern revolvers.

In the 1930s, target shooting became popular to the extent that target type pistols were designed from regular production models. This began a trend that continues to the present day. The features incorporated into a target weapon are usually more advanced than those generally found in common production weapons. In time, these advanced features 'trickle down' into the regular production firearms.

This phenomenon of a shifting awareness that pistols could be used for long range target shooting with great accuracy, and not merely for short range work, and the gradual inclusion of target model features into standard off-the-shelf pistols has laid the foundation for constant improvements in Colt firearms—particularly the revolver series—since the turn of the century.

The history of Colt revolvers from the early 1900s until the mid 1950s is basically a picture of several different models, basically similar to one another, being produced in very large quantities and providing the collectors with an almost insurmountable task of tracing, cataloguing, and documenting this body of firearms. The four standard means of differentiating these different models from one another are noting the size and type of hammer employed, the type of sights, the kind and size of grips, and the barrel and chamber dimensions.

Even employing these methods, the task of documenting different models is sometimes overwhelming. As an ex-

of the Revolver

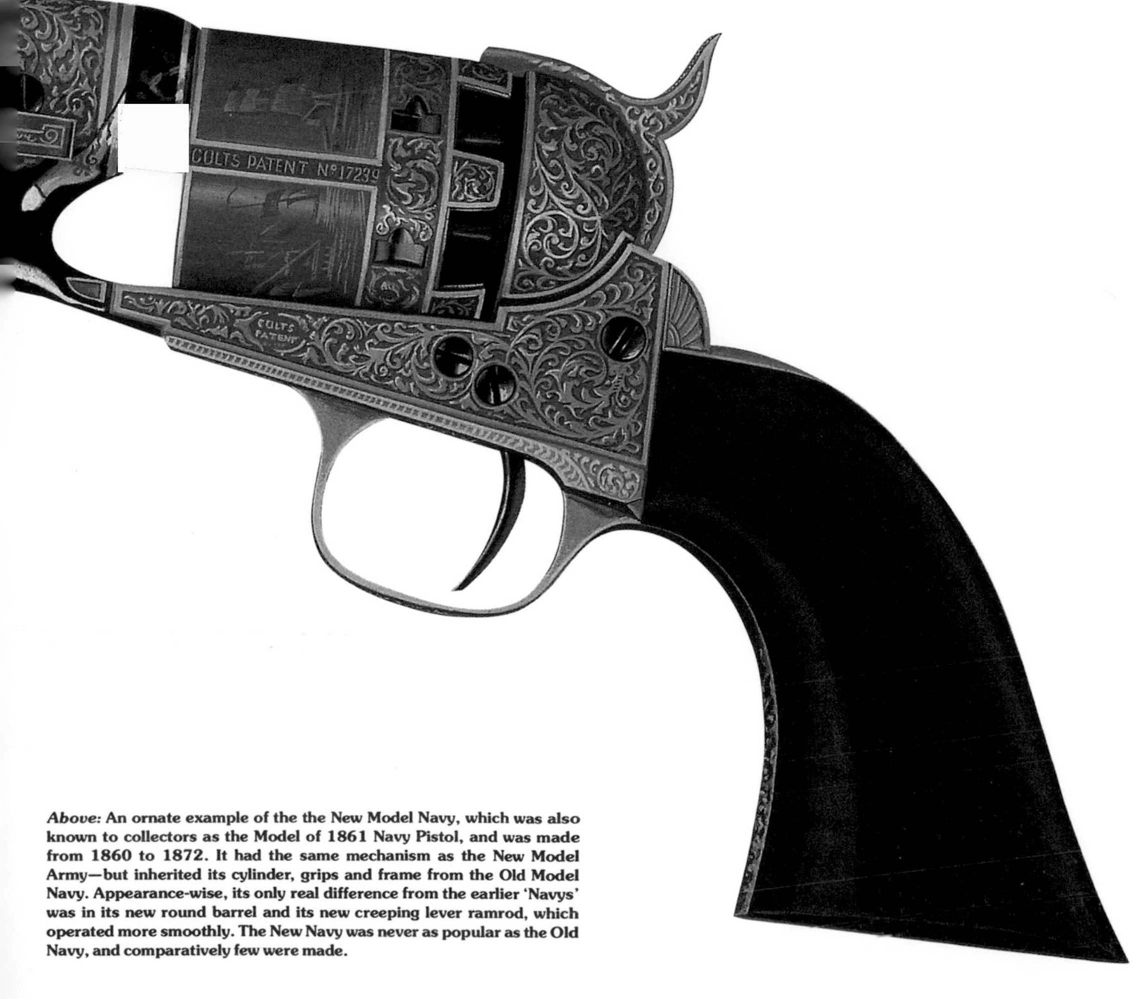

Above: An ornate example of the the New Model Navy, which was also known to collectors as the Model of 1861 Navy Pistol, and was made from 1860 to 1872. It had the same mechanism as the New Model Army—but inherited its cylinder, grips and frame from the Old Model Navy. Appearance-wise, its only real difference from the earlier 'Navys' was in its new round barrel and its new creeping lever ramrod, which operated more smoothly. The New Navy was never as popular as the Old Navy, and comparatively few were made.

ample, the New Service Double Action Revolvers were introduced in 1898. Between then and the middle 1940s, when the model was discontinued, over 350,000 were produced. There were so many serial number runs employed during this time that a collector could specialize in only these New Service Pistols, and probably never be able to acquire a representative specimen of each of the conformations.

It was also during this era that the modern 'snubnosed' pistols gained prominence. In 1837 Samuel Colt had introduced what collectors have since referred to as a 'Baby Paterson Pistol.' It had not proven to be very popular since concealable weapons at that period of American history were not of great importance. But in the 1920s, two snubnosed pistols were introduced into the market place—both of .38 caliber and varying only in barrel lengths. These were the 'Detective Special' and the 'Banker's Special.' Over 400,000 of these particular models have been produced to the present time.

In 1955, the Colt Python came into the hands of eager enthusiasts. This pistol was, and continues to be, the top of Colt's line of revolvers. It is, in the minds of many, without doubt the finest production revolver money can buy. It is available with various grips, triggers, hammers and sights. It is the 'issue weapon' of many police departments around the country. The Python has been the recipient of a veritable galaxy of awards and world records. Every Python, even though produced on an assembly-line basis, both is hand fitted and features the hand honing of all interior and exterior contact points. Pythons feature ventilated ribs, for greater heat dispersion in the barrel, a fast cocking wide spur hammer and a fully shrouded ejecter rod. The .357 Magnum Python uses both .357 Magnum and .38 Special amunition. The Python features a 'locking hand' which secures the cylinder firmly into place when firing—no other double action revolver of any make incorporates this particular feature.

Up until the Python's introduction, the Officers Model .38 Special had been the premier Colt revolver. It had won numerous NRA center-fire pistol championships. These Officers Models were generally customized privately by

Counterclockwise from immediate below: **A 1933 advertisement for the Colt Bankers' Special; two pages from the 1940 Colt catalogue—the New Service Revolver was claimed to be able to stop 'any animal on the American Continent'; the Colt Python, Colt's top of the line revolver, was made available to the general public in 1955.**

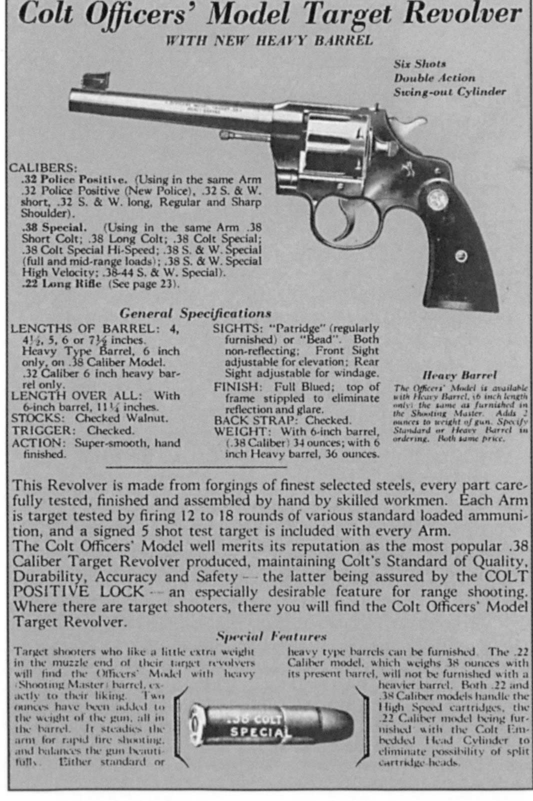

Colt Officers' Model Target Revolver

WITH NEW HEAVY BARREL

Six Shots
Double Action
Swing-out Cylinder

CALIBERS:
.32 Police Positive. (Using in the same Arm .32 Police Positive (New Police), .32 S. & W. short, .32 S. & W. long, Regular and Sharp Shoulder).
.38 Special. (Using in the same Arm .38 Short Colt; .38 Long Colt; .38 Colt Special; .38 Colt Special Hi-Speed; .38 S. & W. Special (full and mid-range loads); .38 S. & W. Special High Velocity; .38-44 S. & W. Special).
.22 Long Rifle (See page 23).

General Specifications

LENGTHS OF BARREL: 4, 4½, 5, 6 or 7½ inches. Heavy Type Barrel, 6 inch only, on .38 Caliber Model. .32 Caliber 6 inch heavy barrel only.
LENGTH OVER ALL: With 6-inch barrel, 11¼ inches.
STOCKS: Checked Walnut.
TRIGGER: Checked.
ACTION: Super-smooth, hand finished.
SIGHTS: "Patridge" (regularly furnished) or "Bead". Both non-reflecting; Front Sight adjustable for elevation; Rear Sight adjustable for windage.
FINISH: Full Blued; top of frame stippled to eliminate reflection and glare.
BACK STRAP: Checked.
WEIGHT: With 6-inch barrel, (.38 Caliber) 34 ounces; with 6 inch Heavy barrel, 36 ounces.

Heavy Barrel

The Officers' Model is available with Heavy Barrel, (6 inch length only) the same as furnished in the Shooting Master. Adds 2 ounces to weight of gun. Specify Standard or Heavy Barrel in ordering. Both same price.

This Revolver is made from forgings of finest selected steels, every part carefully tested, finished and assembled by hand by skilled workmen. Each Arm is target tested by firing 12 to 18 rounds of various standard loaded ammunition, and a signed 5 shot test target is included with every Arm.
The Colt Officers' Model well merits its reputation as the most popular .38 Caliber Target Revolver produced, maintaining Colt's Standard of Quality, Durability, Accuracy and Safety—the latter being assured by the COLT POSITIVE LOCK—an especially desirable feature for range shooting. Where there are target shooters, there you will find the Colt Officers' Model Target Revolver.

Special Features

Target shooters who like a little extra weight in the muzzle end of their target revolvers will find the Officers' Model with heavy (Shooting Master) barrel, exactly to their liking. Two ounces have been added to the weight of the gun, all in the barrel. It steadies the arm for rapid fire shooting, and balances the gun beautifully. Either standard or heavy type barrels can be furnished. The .22 Caliber model, which weighs 38 ounces with its present barrel, will not be furnished with a heavier barrel. Both .22 and .38 Caliber models handle the High Speed cartridges, the .22 Caliber model being furnished with the Colt Embedded Head Cylinder to eliminate possibility of split cartridge-heads.

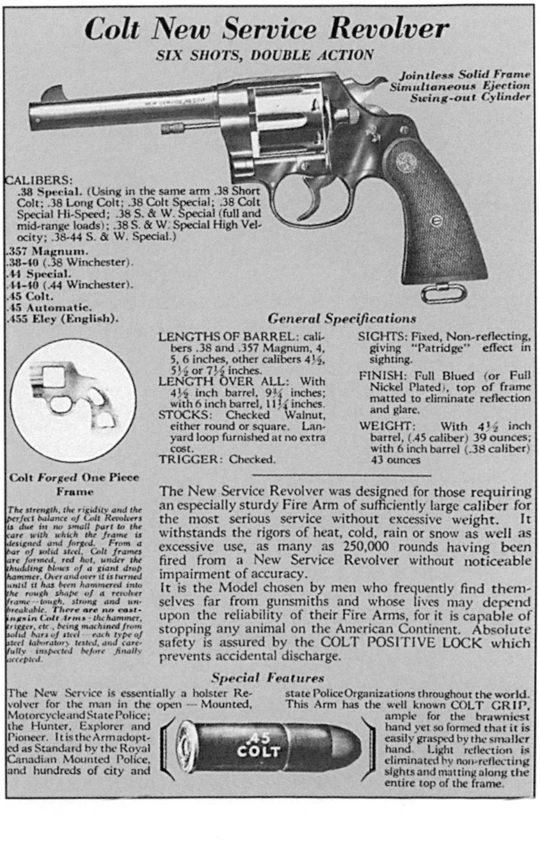

Colt New Service Revolver

SIX SHOTS, DOUBLE ACTION

Jointless Solid Frame
Simultaneous Ejection
Swing-out Cylinder

CALIBERS:
.38 Special. (Using in the same arm .38 Short Colt; .38 Long Colt; .38 Colt Special; .38 Colt Special Hi-Speed; .38 S. & W. Special (full and mid-range loads); .38 S. & W. Special High Velocity; .38-44 S. & W. Special.)
.357 Magnum.
.38-40 (.38 Winchester).
.44 Special.
.44-40 (.44 Winchester).
.45 Colt.
.45 Automatic.
.455 Eley (English).

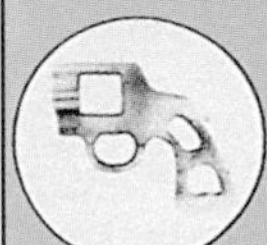

Colt *Forged* One Piece Frame

The strength, the rigidity and the perfect balance of Colt Revolvers is due in no small part to the care with which the frame is designed and forged. From a bar of solid steel, Colt frames are formed, red hot, under the thudding blows of a giant drop hammer. Over and over it is turned until it has been hammered into the rough shape of a revolver frame—tough, strong and unbreakable. ***There are no castings in Colt Arms****—the hammer, trigger, etc., being machined from solid bars of steel—each type of steel laboratory tested, and carefully inspected before finally accepted.*

General Specifications

LENGTHS OF BARREL: calibers .38 and .357 Magnum, 4, 5, 6 inches, other calibers 4½, 5½ or 7½ inches.
LENGTH OVER ALL: With 4½ inch barrel, 9¾ inches; with 6 inch barrel, 11¼ inches.
STOCKS: Checked Walnut, either round or square. Lanyard loop furnished at no extra cost.
TRIGGER: Checked.
SIGHTS: Fixed, Non-reflecting, giving "Patridge" effect in sighting.
FINISH: Full Blued (or Full Nickel Plated), top of frame matted to eliminate reflection and glare.
WEIGHT: With 4½ inch barrel, (.45 caliber) 39 ounces; with 6 inch barrel (.38 caliber) 43 ounces

The New Service Revolver was designed for those requiring an especially sturdy Fire Arm of sufficiently large caliber for the most serious service without excessive weight. It withstands the rigors of heat, cold, rain or snow as well as excessive use, as many as 250,000 rounds having been fired from a New Service Revolver without noticeable impairment of accuracy.
It is the Model chosen by men who frequently find themselves far from gunsmiths and whose lives may depend upon the reliability of their Fire Arms, for it is capable of stopping any animal on the American Continent. Absolute safety is assured by the COLT POSITIVE LOCK which prevents accidental discharge.

Special Features

The New Service is essentially a holster Revolver for the man in the open — Mounted, Motorcycle and State Police; the Hunter, Explorer and Pioneer. It is the Arm adopted as Standard by the Royal Canadian Mounted Police, and hundreds of city and state Police Organizations throughout the world. This Arm has the well known COLT GRIP, ample for the brawniest hand yet so formed that it is easily grasped by the smaller hand. Light reflection is eliminated by non-reflecting sights and matting along the entire top of the frame.

knowledgeable gunsmiths. Ventilated ribs and underslung barrel weights had been added to increase their accuracy.

Even though Smith and Wesson had produced .357 Magnums before the Python appeared, it was Colt's idea to produce a *deluxe* Magnum pistol. The name 'Python' actually came from a contest among Colt factory employees, and not from anyone in the advertising division of the company. Stainless steel Pythons would appear later, but the original Python featured a special finish referred to as Colt Royal Blue. This Royal Blue finish is still the most popular today. It is a concession to the fact that the appearance of beautiful, deep blueing is not a function of the blueing procedure itself as much as it is a process of the polishing—which takes place after the blueing. Royal Blue is achieved by the use of extremely fine grit sand papers and crocus cloths that are used on the exterior parts. The Python took the market by storm, even though it was somewhat more expensive than its competitors, the Smith and Wesson Highway Patrolman, the Combat Magnum, and the Smith and Wesson .357 Magnum. Not only was the finish unexpectedly beautiful, but the internal action of the Python was equally as

COLT
PYTHON .357

At left: The New Service Revolver, made from 1897 to the mid-1940s, was produced in countless variations, and was available in plain and (as shown here) very fancy models. *Below:* A highly engraved Python .357 Magnum with vented barrel rib. *Below left:* A snubnosed stainless steel Python. The Colt Python design is known as the 'Rolls Royce' of revolvers.

astounding. The internal parts of these first Pythons were hand polished, producing an action that was silky smooth and seemingly friction-free.

The Python is a rather heavy pistol, weighing 34 ounces. The weight is distributed more toward the muzzle, thus offering target shooters a balance which results in more accurate sighting of the target in rapid-fire situations. This increased weight also contributes to the Python's ability to absorb recoil even when using large caliber cartridges.

The Python reigns as the 'Rolls Royce' of revolvers and as the hand gun most enthusiasts dream of owning. From the initial machining of its forged frame to its final polishing, through many hours of hand work, the Python is the pinnacle of American gunsmithing today. It is available in four barrel lengths—2.5 inch, four inch, six inch and eight inch. The finishes are Royal Blue with walnut grips, stainless steel and heavily polished Ultimate stainless steel with black Colt neoprene grips. All Pythons are equipped with red insert front sights and adjustable white outline rear sights. The Python can be considered an investment in a precision double action revolver, and it is currently backed by an unprecedented 10 year limited warranty.

Today, Colt firearms carries on a tradition of innovation stretching back 150 years. Even with sophisticated techniques such as laser bore sighting, the bedrock of Colt's quality still rests in the skilled hands of its craftsmen, working with the timeless strength of forged steel. In 1986, the Custom Shop at Colt undertook its most expansive project in the 150 years of Colt's existence. The 150th Anniversary Exhibition Model, a .45 caliber Colt single action one-of-a-kind Army Model Pistol was auctioned at a black tie affair in Las Vegas in 1986. This revolver is heavily embellished with gold inlaid motifs, border bands, and scroll work. It is appropriately serial numbered 'Colt-150.' The genuine hand carved ivory grips are enhanced by a solid gold butt cap depicting a patriotic eagle, with a small diamond being the eagle's eye. Included with this pistol was a custom designed, solid ebony and cocobolo-wood presentation case with an ivory hand carved Colt medallion insert. Even a leather bound scrapbook, detailing its 1986 Exhibition Tour and a museum quality exhibition case were included. Starting price for the bidding was set at $150,000.00!

Fortunately, one did not have to be invited to the black tie auction in Las Vegas in order to purchase an 'Anniversary Commemorative Colt Pistol.' An 'Anniversary Engraving Sampler' was offered to all Colt customers who purchased a currently-produced blue or nickel finished gun in 1986. This 'Engraving Sampler' was a unique concept, in that the

Collectors' items—Although Colt's 150th Anniversary Exhibition Gun *(opposite)* had a $150,000 auction price tag, a humble old Single Action Army Frontier Model similar to the one *below* (but with serial number 1) fetched $242,000 at an auction at Christie's East in 1981.

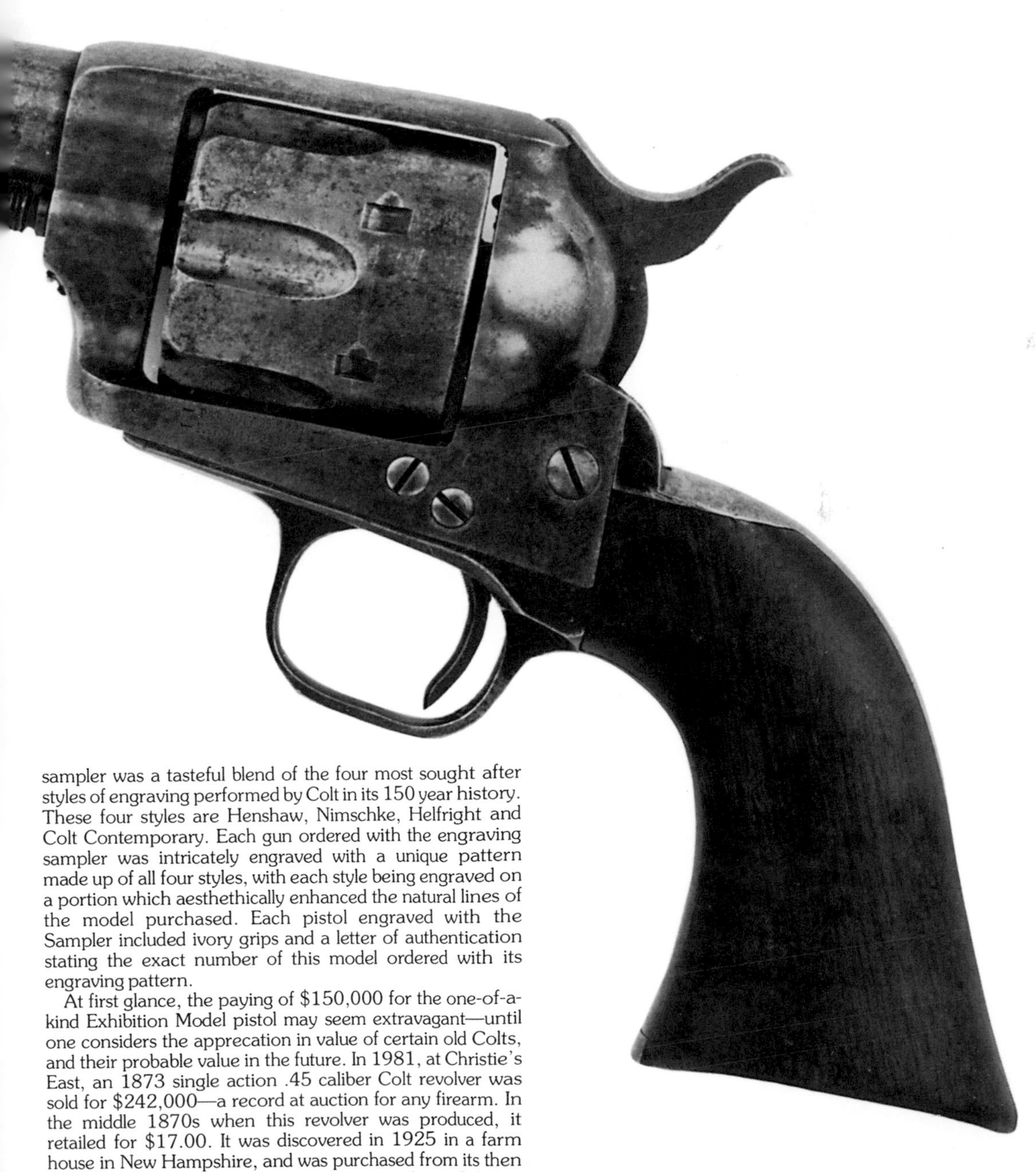

sampler was a tasteful blend of the four most sought after styles of engraving performed by Colt in its 150 year history. These four styles are Henshaw, Nimschke, Helfright and Colt Contemporary. Each gun ordered with the engraving sampler was intricately engraved with a unique pattern made up of all four styles, with each style being engraved on a portion which aesthethically enhanced the natural lines of the model purchased. Each pistol engraved with the Sampler included ivory grips and a letter of authentication stating the exact number of this model ordered with its engraving pattern.

At first glance, the paying of $150,000 for the one-of-a-kind Exhibition Model pistol may seem extravagant—until one considers the apprecation in value of certain old Colts, and their probable value in the future. In 1981, at Christie's East, an 1873 single action .45 caliber Colt revolver was sold for $242,000—a record at auction for any firearm. In the middle 1870s when this revolver was produced, it retailed for $17.00. It was discovered in 1925 in a farm house in New Hampshire, and was purchased from its then owner for $4.00. It is staggering to imagine what a Colt Anniversary Pistol may be worth 20 or 30 years from now.

Automatic and

Colt Automatic Pistol

POCKET MODEL, HAMMERLESS
CALIBERS .32 AND .380

For the Following Cartridges:
Caliber .32 Rimless, Smokeless.
Caliber .380 Rimless, Smokeless.

CAPACITY OF MAGAZINE.
Cal. .32, 8 shots.
Cal. .380, 7 shots.

LENGTH OF BARREL. 3¾ inches.

FINISH. Full Blued or Full Nickel Plated
Checked Walnut Stocks.

WEIGHT. 23 ounces.

LENGTH OVER ALL. 6¾ inches.

This popular Colt Automatic Pistol is a light, well balanced arm; powerful, yet convenient as a personal weapon. Hammerless with a solid breech construction there are no projecting parts, making the arm convenient and dependable for protection. Accidental discharge is made impossible by the Slide Lock as well as the COLT AUTOMATIC GRIP SAFETY. The Slide Lock is thrown on or off by the thumb and not only disconnects the trigger from the operating mechanism but serves as an indicator, showing whether the arm is cocked or not. THE GRIP SAFETY is entirely automatic in operation, locking the mechanism until the pistol is firmly grasped at time of discharge. These two positive safeties absolutely prevent any accidental discharge. In addition, the Caliber .32 from No. [illegible] and Caliber .380 from No. [illegible] are now equipped with a Safety Disconnector similar to that incorporated in the Caliber .25 as described under that model.

At top: **A neat and handy Pocket Model Colt Hammerless Automatic Pistol, circa 1940, and *(above)* a 1926 ad for same from Colt's catalogue.**

Pistols Rifles

The invention in the latter 19th century of a new type of gunpowder caused a revolution in ballistics circles. This new powder burned much more efficiently than did black powder. You could pack more punch into a smaller cartridge, and all sorts of interesting things could be done with larger cartridges. Firearms had to be manufactured with more stress capacity to handle this hot new stuff, and therefore arms technology *really* started to take off. This new powder, incidentally, didn't stink the place up so much as did black powder, and it was called 'smokeless powder.'

The principle of any automatic weapon is very simple. When the initial cartridge is fired, the natural recoil from the explosion is used to do two things—namely, eject the spent shell and reload a new cartridge into the chamber. A 'fully' automatic weapon is one in which only one trigger depression is needed to set off a simultaneous series of shots. The designation 'semi-automatic' is used to differentiate the action from a 'fully-automatic' one in that a 'semi-automatic' will fire, eject and reload only one cartridge per trigger pull. A further differentiation between automatic-type weapons can be made on the basis of whether the energy used to eject the spent cartridge and reload the new one is derived from recoil, or whether it is derived from utilizing expanded gases which are released during the detonation. Most automatic weapons are of the recoil type operation, whereas some larger machine guns are operated on the gas expansion basis.

John M Browning, of Browning Arms fame, is credited with originating the idea of firearms that could load and unload themselves. In experiments in the early 1890s, Browning noticed that when a gun was fired, not only did the projectile fly out of the end of the barrel, but gases were released out that same opening. Browning noticed this phenomenon when he observed that as a gun is fired in close proximity to tall grasses or weeds, the explosion violently disturbs the adjacent foilage. He concluded that there must be some way of utilizing that otherwise wasted energy.

The principle of rapid fire guns, at least, was nothing new to Colt Firearms. From the middle 1860's, Colt had produced the famous Gatling gun. These 10-barreled guns could fire 600 rounds per minute of .45-70 cartridges. But of course, their power to fire at such rates was entirely dependent on the human muscle of the operater. Still, the Gatling guns were the best of the rapid-fire weapons for many years.

John Browning concluded that since Colt was at the forefront of rapid-fire weapons, they would be most interested in his ideas and patents. He was right. In 1895 the Colt/Browning Automatic Gun was brought to the marketplace. This tripod-mounted, air-cooled and belt fed machine gun could fire 400 shots per minute. It was used to great advantage in both the Spanish-American War and in World War I. But, obviously, these kinds of weapons were not intended for the general public. This, however, did not preclude the general populace from wanting handguns that operated on this same automatic principle.

Colt became the first American manufacturer of an automatic pistol in 1900. The Model 1900 was a .38 caliber weapon weighing 37 ounces, having a barrel six inches in length and a magazine capacity of seven shots. These seven shots were of a new straight-cased .38 caliber rimless cartridge that was capable of a velocity of 1260 feet per second—a truly astounding speed for the times. The Model 1900, even though it was manufactured by Colt, was in fact based on the 1897 patents of the Browning Arms Company. On 20 April, 1897, Browning filed a series of four patents which were to remain the benchmarks of automatic

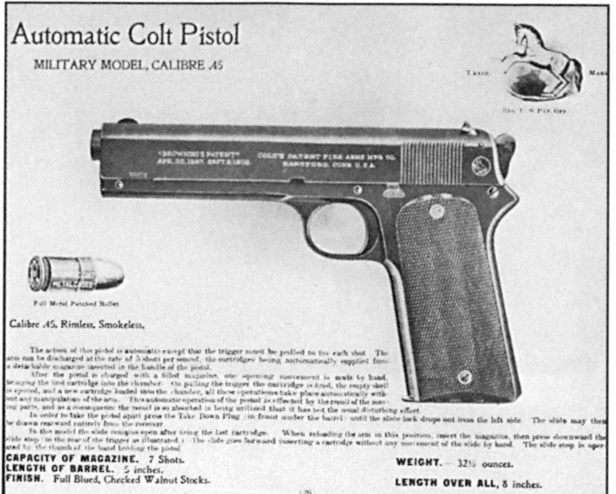

Automatic Colt Pistol

MILITARY MODEL, CALIBRE .45

Full Metal Patched Bullet

Calibre .45, Rimless, Smokeless.

The action of this pistol is automatic except that the trigger must be pulled to fire each shot. The arm can be discharged at the rate of 5 shots per second, the cartridges being automatically supplied from a detachable magazine inserted in the handle of the pistol.

After the pistol is charged with a filled magazine, one opening movement is made by hand, bringing the first cartridge into the chamber. On pulling the trigger the cartridge is fired, the empty shell is ejected, and a new cartridge loaded into the chamber, all these operations take place automatically without any manipulation of the arm. This automatic operation of the pistol is effected by the recoil of the moving parts, and as a consequence the recoil is so absorbed in being utilized that it has not the usual disturbing effect.

In order to take the pistol apart press the Take Down Plug (in front under the barrel) until the slide lock drops out from the left side. The slide may then be drawn rearward entirely from the receiver.

In this model the slide remains open after firing the last cartridge. When reloading the arm in this position, insert the magazine, then press downward the slide stop (to the rear of the trigger as illustrated). The slide goes forward inserting a cartridge without any movement of the slide by hand. The slide stop is operated by the thumb of the hand holding the pistol.

CAPACITY OF MAGAZINE. 7 Shots.
LENGTH OF BARREL. 5 inches.
FINISH. Full Blued, Checked Walnut Stocks.

WEIGHT. — 32½ ounces.

LENGTH OVER ALL, 8 inches.

(20)

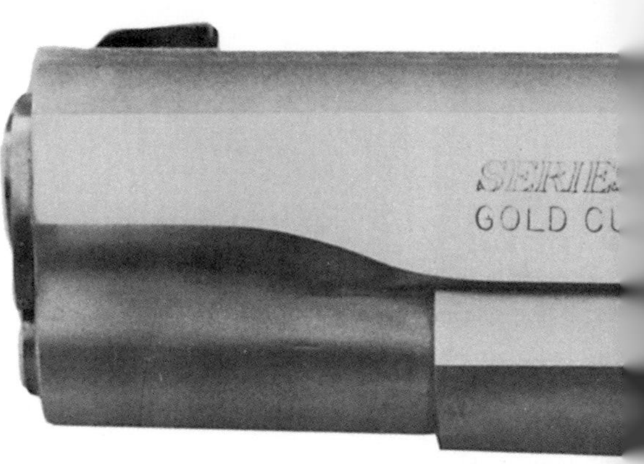

pistols into the 1940s. Indeed, the date of 'April 20' was so important that it was imprinted onto each weapon for many years. Many innovations followed with succeeding models coming out in 1902, 1903, 1905, 1907, 1908 and 1911. This time frame, from 1897 until 1911, is accounted by many to be one of the most innovative and creative periods in Colt's history. This combination of Browning's originality and Colt's precision manufacturing set down the basics for automatic weapons to this day.

Calibrations for Colt automatic pistols are much simpler than for Colt revolvers. Only .22 rimfire, .25, .32, .380, .38, .38 Special, Super .38, 9mm, .45 and .455 have been produced.

An interesting abbreviation appears beside certain calibers of automatic weapons. This abbreviation, 'ACP,' stands for Automatic Colt Pistol. The 'ACP' shell casings differ from other cartridges in that there is a reduced indenture of rim at the rear of the cartridge. This is to enable the cartridge to be quickly loaded and ejected by the automatic weapon's mechanism.

It is interesting, and somewhat humorous, to note that when the Model 1900 came out, the first people to shoot it had a difficult time getting used to the automatic character of the weapon. Generally, when a person began shooting an automatic pistol, because he did not know what to expect out of this device, his shots were generally far from accurate (to say the least). The Great Unknown was very disquieting to those first automatic shooters. But one quickly caught on to the tremendous advantages of an automatically loading and ejecting weapon. The 'trigger finger' had been rediscovered as a vital part of the human anatomy!

When the first prototype of the Model 1900 was submitted to the US Ordnance Board, their tests proved somewhat inconclusive. The Board stated that, 'This type of pistol has not yet reached such a stage as to justify its adoption in the place of the revolver for Service use.' Reliability was the key question involved in whether the government should abandon the revolver as the military's sidearm weapon of issue and go with the new automatic.

In time, however, the Colt automatic was adopted by the military. Of the 4.7 million Colt automatic pistols that have been produced, the US Government has been the purchaser of at least three million of them. While many different models of automatic pistols have been, and still are, produced by Colt with numberless variations among these different basic styles, the model 1911 and the 1911 A-l still rank as the company's best selling automatics.

Currently, the Gold Cup National Match Mark IV Series 80 is the top of the line Colt automatic pistol. It has a barrel length of five inches and weighs 39 ounces. The Gold Cup is

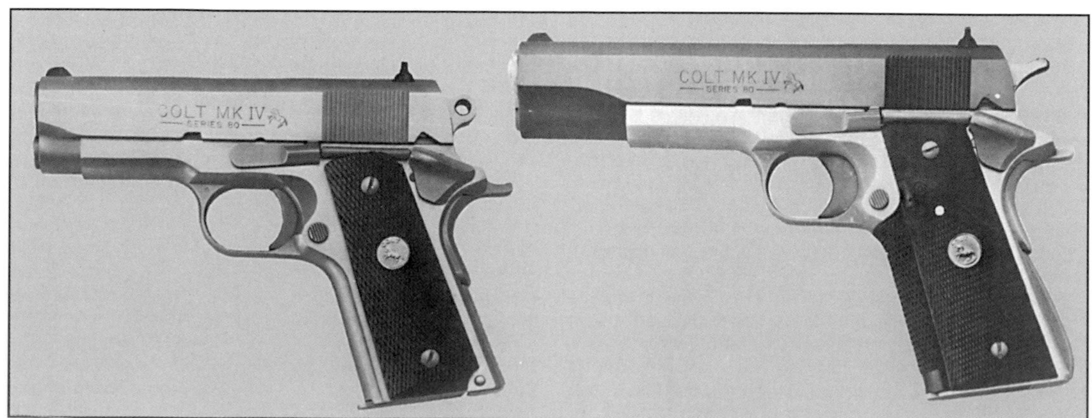

the premier American center-fire automatic target pistol, with its accurizor barrel that tightens shot groupings by as much as 90 percent. This Colt automatic is acclaimed as one of the world's finest match scorers. It features a wide grooved trigger with an adjustable top, serrated target hammer, and flat back-strap mainspring housing. It also features the revolutionary Firing Pin Safety, which allows the bearer to carry a round in the chamber in the 'cocked and locked' position—which enables the shooter to deliver consistent trigger pull on all shots, rather than the heavy first pull of a double action.

From its historic beginnings, Colt has continued to improve its line of automatic pistols to include, *clockwise from left:* the Stainless Steel Gold Cup National Match; the MK IV Combat Elite Series 80; the MK IV Stainless Steel Officer's model; MK IV Series 80 Gold Cup National Match; and a 1905 advertisement which states that the Automatic Colt Pistol is 'automatic except that the trigger must be pulled to fire each shot.'

PATENTED APR 20 1897. SEPT. 9 1902.
DEC 19 1905. FEB 14. 1911. AUG. 19. 1913

Above: **A fancy civilian version of the Colt 1911 Model Automatic Pistol, which has for years been the standard sidearm for the US military. *At left:* The terror of latter-19th century military encounters was the manually-cranked Gatling Gun, which Colt produced to the design specs of the Gun's inventor, Dr Gatling (far left).**

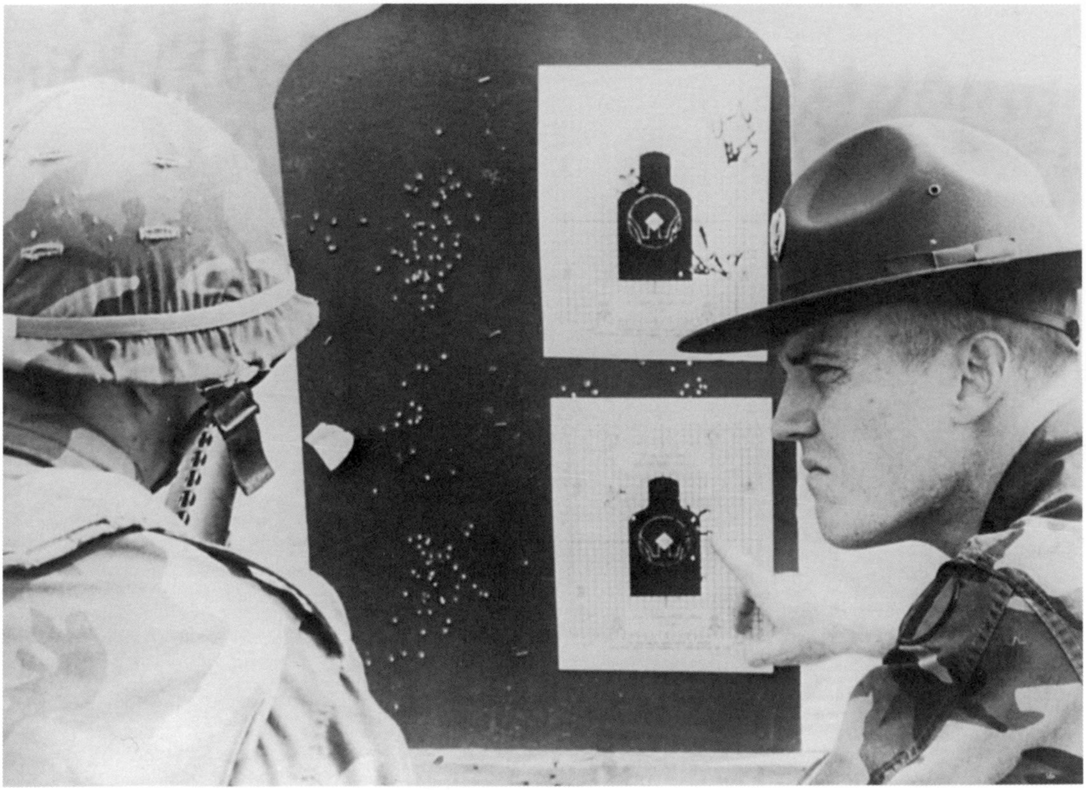

***Above:* This drill sergeant shows a soldier how to 'zero in' his M16 for better accuracy. *Below:* An AR-15 A2 Sporter II—one variant of its military cousin, the M16. *Opposite:* US Marines and their M16s, on guard at the terrorist-bombed US embassy in Beirut, in the early 1980s.**

Undoubtedly, the most famous of Colt's automatic weapons are the AR-15 and M16 Automatic and semi-automatic rifles. The caliber of these rifles is .223.

In the early 1960s, Colt acquired the rights to produce and market the AR-15 rifle from the Armalite Division of the Fairchild Engine and Airplane Corporation. Colt Arms had the connections necessary to place this rifle, in large quantities, into the hands of both law enforcement and government officials. The US Army began contracting for these rifles in 1963, partly at the request of General Curtis LeMay. As US involvement in Southeast Asia increased and the war in Vietnam began to unfold in ever greater ferocity, more and more AR-15 rifles were ordered by the government. So many AR-15s were put on the front lines that the weapon was adopted as the replacement for the then-standard M14 rifle. Because the AR-15 replaced the M14, its name was changed to the M16. Today, however, the designation AR-15 is still to be found on the civilian version of this military weapon known as the Sporter.

As the M16 found its way into different environments of hostilities, variations were produced in accordance with need. Today the M16 is available in carbine, heavy assault rifle, submachine gun, light machine gun and survival pack models, and even is equipable as a grenade launcher.

Colt Industries spent literally millions of dollars in plant production equipment for the M16 as well as a new test range complex built in West Hartford, Connecticut. Even foreign plants are licensed by Colt for the protection of the M16 in Korea, the Philippines and Indonesia. Few products of any type or variety produced by any manufacturer have enjoyed the ready recognizability of the Colt-made M16 Automatic Rifle.

Craftsmanship Twentieth

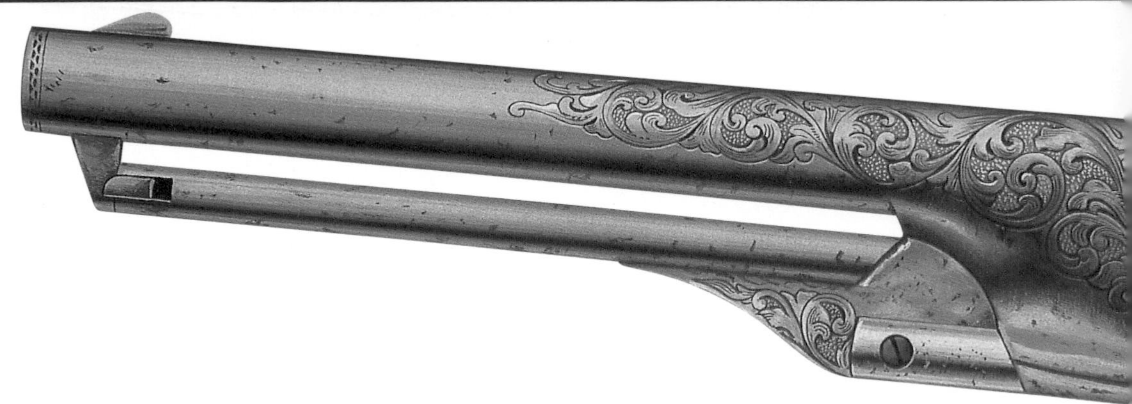

The following account, in the form of a tour of Colt's Hartford, Connecticut, factory, was originally published in 1940 in *A Century of Achievement*. The insights contained here are as good a view into the heart and soul of Colt's commitment to craftsmanship as they are into the factory itself. Though this selection may be from another time, the spirit and commitment are still alive and well, such that it could have been written yesterday.

Because raw steel is such a vital factor in the production of a firearm, the greatest care is given to its selection. Before a machine even touches it, the steel itself must conform to the most rigid of specifications.

Steel mills have on their order files the specifications which Colt metallurgists have laid down as the kind of steel they want. In a New Jersey mill, a quantity of steel is being made. It is given a heat number. Billet samples of this raw steel before it is rolled into shape are sent to the Colt factory for approval. To the laboratory it goes. It is given a Brinell test to determine its hardness, which is another way to say whether it is machineable or not. Too soft, it will tear; too hard, it will ruin the cutters.

The billet samples are submitted to chemical and physical inspections. They are acid etched to reveal defects. They are fractured three separate times: first for grain size; then hardened, tested for hardness and fractured a second time as hard; and as a final test to determine their toughness, they are drawn and then fractured as drawn.

If the billet samples are OK'd, the steel mill is notified that the particular heat number has been approved and to proceed to roll the steel into the specific pieces and sizes on order by Colt. Steel men often say that the Colt people are 'almost unreasonable' in their demands.

From the steel sheds and laboratory, the forging shop is our first stop. A blank is heated red hot. With long tongs it is placed on the forge. A giant weight, released by the mechanism of a foot pedal, forges the steel between the two dies into shape. Literally it pounds the molecules of steel into the desired shape. I watch the frame of my revolver drop forged into a jointless solid piece. It's a terrifying sight, this drop forging. The drop die weighs between 500 and 600 pounds. It drops six feet exerting a force of over 2000 pounds. Sparks fly 10 or 12 feet when the die hits the steel. The terrific heat and the earsplitting noise conjures an image in the mind of some gigantic monster giving full vent to its fury. Across the alley from the forge shop a battery of punch presses trim off the excess metal resulting from the forging. The trimmed pieces are next placed into a steel drum and shot blasted to smooth their surfaces. We open one of the drums where a number of pistol receivers are tumbling. The term 'shot blasting' is well named. Under heavy air pressure a veritable shower of fine steel shot is blasted over all the surfaces, removing all scale.

Down go the forgings to the grinding room. Each individual receiver or frame is set on a heavily magnetized chuck to hold it tightly in place, and is forced between seg-

in the Century

At top: This heavily-engraved New Model Navy Pistol is evidence of the long Colt tradition of craftsmanly care. *Above:* The Colt armory on the banks of the Connecticut River, in the 1940s.

Colt firearms, such as the Peacekeeper at *above right*, must meet exacting standards. *Immediate right:* Arms expert JH Fitzgerald. *Above:* Colt's Forge Shop—where frames were swaged from solid bars of steel—in the 1940s. *Below:* Heat treating ovens. *Opposite:* Profiling machines.

mented wheels of carborundum whirling in opposite directions. Each piece is ground to the proper thickness, and the top and bottom surfaces are made smooth.

Masters Of Steel

There is probably no more important department in the whole Colt plant than the heat treating room. In this room filled with roaring furnaces, the varying conditions of steel are mastered. Steel is made softer, harder, drawn to fine temper and in a number of ways processed to fit the exact needs that will be demanded of it. For instance, the drop forgings must be normalized before they can be machined. Normalizing the forging prepares the steel so that it can be machined with maximum efficiency—not too soft, not too hard. When all the machining processes are completed, the same pieces are hardened again. Take the slide of an automatic, as an example: it takes a terrible beating. It has to travel back and forth on the receiver every time a shot is fired. Innumerable machine operations are necessary—60 to be exact. After each slide has gone through its machining routine, it is sent back again to the heat treating room to be heat treated. The same thing holds true of barrels and cylinders. Triggers, cranes, latches, sears, firing pins, hammers and etc are also hardened in the heat treating room.

Built Like a Watch But Strong Enough To Stand Dynamite

The number of different and separate machine operations that go into the production of a Colt revolver or automatic pistol is simply staggering.

In the factory office of Mr Harry Stevens, the assistant works manager, is a library of several volumes, each containing a thorough description of all the various and sundry factory operations. There is a whole volume, for instance, describing in detail in sucessive numerical order each and every operation on a Colt Officers' Model Target Revolver. Another covers the 'S' Model which you and I know as the Woodsman .22 Long Rifle Automatic Pistol—incidentally, as sweet a little .22 as ever felt the squeeze of a hand. But let me stick to my story.

In every foreman's office are duplicates of these master factory control books, each foreman having that part which comes under his jurisdiction. Operation Number 86, for example, in the manufacture of a Government Model .45 receiver is to 'hand finish recoil spring hold, slideways, magazine opening and mainspring housing cuts.'

Believe it or not, there are some 1400 separate operations in making a Colt revolver. There are about 1200 separate operations in manufacturing a Colt automatic pistol.

Obviously it would be impossible to attempt to describe any real portion of them. Even if I tried, you would soon get

lost in a maze of technical detail. And so would I. The most I can do is to describe a few important operations such as rifling the barrel, drilling the cylinders, filing, fitting, assembling, testing, finishing, blueing… major operations that call for departments of their own.

'Fitz' guides me to one of the big machine rooms. Revolvers and automatics are not made on the same machines. The machine operations on a revolver are in charge of Timothy Trant; the machine operations of an automatic are under the supervision of Britthold Magnusson. We toss a coin to see which we'll go through. Heads it is—Trant wins.

In geometrical arrangement, hundreds of machines are spaced in this great room. Huge batteries of them stretch in rows from one side of the room to the other. Machines are grouped so that, as one operation is complete, the machine to do the following operation is right at hand. Rough and finish milling machines, for example, are side by side. It's really a beautiful sight to watch these hundreds of machines going full blast.

One is immediately aware that careful planning preceded this wonderfully efficient system. Yet such is the history of all progressive manufacturing. You or I go into a plant for the first time. What we see—the efficient layout of machinery, the efficient transportation of power to run those machines, provision made for retooling the machines—are the results of years of planning, of painstaking research, of training and experience. It is so easy and so human to accept all of it with one casual glance without stopping to realize the brains and the energy that were its conception and development.

A frame—drop forged, shot blasted, normalized and ground—comes up to the South Armory, third floor. Immediately, before a single operation is begun, each frame is carefully inspected. Thirty of them are placed on a rack. From then on, each rack goes through as a unit of production.

The first machine operation on a revolver frame is to sidemill it. Next, an especially designed machine shaves out the opening in the frame where the cylinder will eventually

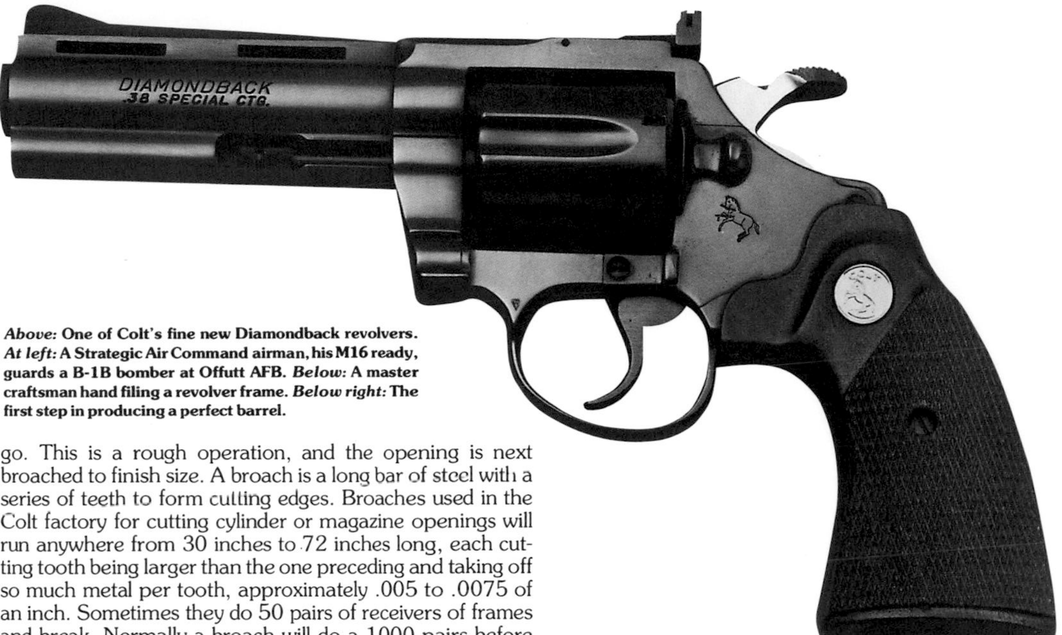

***Above:* One of Colt's fine new Diamondback revolvers. *At left:* A Strategic Air Command airman, his M16 ready, guards a B-1B bomber at Offutt AFB. *Below:* A master craftsman hand filing a revolver frame. *Below right:* The first step in producing a perfect barrel.**

go. This is a rough operation, and the opening is next broached to finish size. A broach is a long bar of steel with a series of teeth to form cutting edges. Broaches used in the Colt factory for cutting cylinder or magazine openings will run anywhere from 30 inches to 72 inches long, each cutting tooth being larger than the one preceding and taking off so much metal per tooth, approximately .005 to .0075 of an inch. Sometimes they do 50 pairs of receivers of frames and break. Normally a broach will do a 1000 pairs before wearing out. Edges, of course, must constantly be honed and kept in the sharpest condition.

After broaching, the second side is first rough milled, then finish milled as was the first side. The frame next goes to a profiling machine. A profiling machine is to steel what a shaper is to wood-working. The cutting tool follows a pattern, milling away the metal to form the shapes desired. It is an interesting operation to watch, for one quickly sees the dropforged blank take shape. Drilling the crane hole is next. After drilling, the hole is reamed and counterbored. The operation is a fussy one, the gauge allowing a tolerance of only .001 of an inch. The barrel hole is next drilled, rough and finish reamed, counterbored, threaded and counterbored again. The frame is placed in a drill chuck again and screw and pin holes are bored. The hammer slot is cut.

The trigger hole is cut. A large hole is then cut on the side of the frame… a chunk is literally taken out. There's a lot of work to do on a revolver frame that's beneath the surface (really, inside the frame)… milling that must be done to make room for the working parts that, when the revolver is complete, are hidden underneath the side plate.

More profiling, more contour cutting… profiling for hammer and trigger, profiling inside stocks, profiling for bolt clearance, profiling the trigger guard. More drilling… firing pin hole, recess for recoil plate. And so it goes—through the 145 separate machine operations that go to make a revolver frame.

'Go' and 'No go'—that's what the gauges read. And believe me, mister, that's just what they mean. The operations must stay within these limitations or else. 'No go' means just that… a fast trip to the scrap pile. Split a hair six times, and you have some idea of the tolerances allowed in certain operations… limitations that permit a difference of only .0005 of an inch. Of course not all tolerances are as exacting as this. Some allow .001 of an inch, some .002, a few as high as .003 of an inch. That's pretty accurate, too. Remember that many parts go into a firearm, which is a

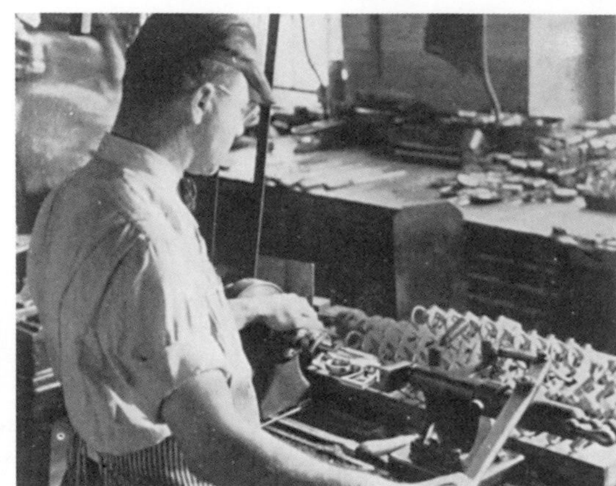

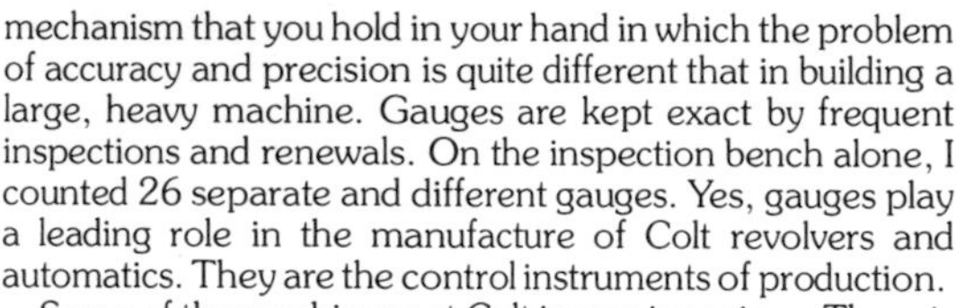

mechanism that you hold in your hand in which the problem of accuracy and precision is quite different that in building a large, heavy machine. Gauges are kept exact by frequent inspections and renewals. On the inspection bench alone, I counted 26 separate and different gauges. Yes, gauges play a leading role in the manufacture of Colt revolvers and automatics. They are the control instruments of production.

Some of the machinery at Colt is very ingenious. There is the regular run of lathes, shapers, drilling machines and etc, but scattered among the conventional machinery are a great many original machines, invented, designed and built in the Colt factory… machines that have no duplicates anywhere in the world. I saw a number of veteran machines that were built many, many years ago still in operation doing their work with efficiency and dispatch.

If you would see an interesting sight, stand on the threshold of one of the huge machine floors in a wing of the Colt factory. There you will see hundreds of machines nestled closely side by side as far as your eye can see. Noisy, yes—but a thrilling sight.

The Magic Touch Of Hands

Hand filing is a very important step in the manufacture of a Colt firearm. On a slide and receiver of an automatic pistol some 40 separate hand filing operations are necessary. On one operation alone I saw 12 different files used, varying in coarseness from one to four. Files of all kinds littered the benches. Many of them looked alike to me, but each had its purpose and each was used for that purpose. The bench jigs that have been designed to hold the various pieces to be filed are very ingenious.

Fitting a slide to a receiver so that it travels easily, yet has no side play, requires filing skill. If a slide rubs a mite, the high spot is filed down. The slide must work freely without shaking. Filing, as with every operation, is inspected and checked. Handfitted slides and receivers are matched and given serial numbers. In the inspection, the serial numbers are checked to be sure that the receiver and slide have the same numbers.

The smooth yet tight fit of the crane to the revolver frame is another filing operation that demands a masterly touch. It must swing easily, yet be snug. So is the fitting of the hammer—that it may work easily between the frame sides. Filing requires the utmost skill. Most Colt filers have been at their benches for a dozen years or more. They are aristocrats of hand work.

Gauging the height of the firing pin is an operation that demands years of experience. Another is filing the sides of the tang for grips. These must be filed so accurately that light cannot show under the center, otherwise there would be a slight rock when the grips were attached. Fittings are so tailored to each gun that once fitted, they are mated so that there can be no chance of their becoming separated. Important fittings such as cranes, side plates and hammers are individually marked by the fitter, who stamps on them his number—forever identifying his handiwork and imposing on him the responsibility of super accurate work.

Making Colt Barrels

Drilling the barrel hole is a continuous process. A flow of oil of 500 pounds pressure forces the fine chips out as fast as the cutting edge takes them off. The drilling process is delicate. It takes about 10 minutes to drill a five inch barrel. One can honestly say that a Colt barrel 'gets a lot of reaming.' A barrel is machine reamed many times, each reaming making the barrel hole a thousandth or so larger.

Since every barrel tapers inside slightly toward the muzzle end, a generous amount of finish reaming is necessary. The target .38, for instance, must come within half a thousandth

Above: A soldier in basic training with his M16. _At right:_ General George Patton with his ivory-handled Colt. In the pistol factory—counterclockwise from _above left_: Ensuring that the barrel lines up correctly; 'proof-testing' the barrel; and chambering the cylinder.

of the exact diameter. Sometimes it is necessary to finish ream a barrel four or five times to acquire this exactness. All along the line, I hold up to the light the barrel that is going into the gun they're building for me. Now they are putting it through the leading and polishing operation. They squirt on a drop or two of hot lead and wipe it through. The hot lead takes out any microscopic ridges and gives the inside of the barrel a high polish. We go to a rifling machine. In rifling, Colt acknowledges no superior. Inserted into the machine, the barrel is rifled. It takes about 20 minutes. Two barrels are on the same machine, each taking its turn as the cam throws the barrel over for its next cut. I hold it to the light again and see a spiral ribbon exactly .0035 deep, a lefthand twist that will spin a bullet accurately to its mark. It is a beautiful sight. No other word describes it.

A lathe turns the outside to exact dimension. The micrometer allows a tolerance of but .002 of an inch. Beyond this tolerance the barrel goes to the scrap heap. And let me say right here lest there be any doubt in your mind, there is a scrap heap at Colt's—never a big one, thanks to efficient workmen carefully supervised. But if there's the slightest doubt as to a tiny flaw or to the accuracy of a given measurement, out the piece goes right then and there. The Colt people bend over backward on this. They demand and they get perfection. A slot is cut and the front sight fitted, wound into place by a brass wire. In a subsequent brazing

Above: A highly-embellished version of the New Model Army Pistol, which was made from about 1860 to 1872. Collectors have since called it the Model of 1860 Army Revolver or the Round-Barreled Army—of the new series of percussion cap revolvers, the Army was the largest. *At left:* Soldiers of the 82nd Airborne gather around a flag during a pause in the action in Grenada; they carried the day with their M16s.

and heat treating process this wire melts in such a manner as to fix the sight as firmly as if it were part of the barrel itself.

Making The Cylinders

There are 60 separate operations on the cylinder alone. Colt cylinders originate from a solid round bar of specification steel. To the layman, this bar of steel looks like a pipe. It is fed into a wonderfully ingenious machine—an automatic machine which cuts the bar to working length. It is an old machine, built by Colt inventors and mechanics some 40 years ago, but it can be dependably counted on to do its work with accuracy that must have been marvelled at at the time the machine was made. The center hole is bored, first rough bored, finish bored, then reamed three times. It must be accurate to .0005 of an inch. Inspectors look each cylinder over to detect any possible flaw in the steel. It is then ground to finish diameter, the diameter gauge allowing a tolerance of less than .002 of an inch. It is then gauged for trueness of diameter, the gauging showing up any slight eccentricity that might have occurred should any particles of dirt have crept into the arbor upon which the cylinder is held while being ground.

Drilling The Chambers

A lathe operation next cuts the cylinder to exact length. Into a drill jig it goes and the six holes are spotted. The bores of the cylinder are drilled half way through from the rear. Then the bores are drilled from the front to complete the process. There is a difference of .0012 between the front and rear ends of the chamber bores. The bores are reamed, first by a boring reamer, then by hand. A milling machine then makes the lightening cuts—the sleeve-like semi-round cuts that you see on the outside of your cylinder at the front end—so-called because their sole purpose is to take out unnecessary weight. Lead cuts are then made to facilitate travel. A coupling is doweled into position. A ratchet rod and ratchet are assembled to the cylinder, and two dowel pins inserted to hold the ratchet in correct and permanent position.

Practically all that remains to complete the cylinder is the fine reaming of the chamber bores. And when I say 'fine reaming,' that is just what I mean. There is no finer industrial reaming done anywhere in the country. The gauges allow no tolerances whatever. Measurements must be held exact to size. Cylinders, all machine operations complete, are sent to the heat treating room for heat treating.

All Colt cylinders turn right: this motion holds the crane tightly against the frame, keeping the chamber and barrel in perfect alignment for every shot.

Fitting And Assembling

From machines to hand filing, to finishing, blueing, assembly, targeting, inspection and finally to stock, is the itinerary of a Colt revolver. Minor machine operations are done en route such as chamfering edges of hammer and trigger slots, gauging fitting stops so that the cylinder will not swing out too far, cutting the safety latch slot and cutting threads inside the frame barrel hole to exact gauge depth and tapering them.

Fitting the cylinder to the frame is an operation assigned only to an expert. Fine files and emery grit are his tools. One man has been fitting cylinders for over 25 years. That has

Opposite: Ranging the barrel and chamber of a Colt revolver, circa 1940. This experienced craftsman had been, as of this photo, on the job for 31 years. *At left:* A Colt Stainless Steel King Cobra .357 Magnum revolver. *Above:* A Delta Elite 10mm Auto pistol. By combining the proven design and reliability of the famous Government Model with a versatile 10mm auto cartridge, the Delta Elite is a highly effective and handy weapon for a variety of applications.

***Above, from bottom:* Stainless steel Officer's ACP; blue Combat Commander; and stainless steel Government Model. *At right, from bottom:* A King Cobra, with short hammer throw for quicker lock time; a Colt Peacekeeper for police work; and the much-renowned Python.**

been his one job—nothing else. He has never worked in any other department.

Facing the barrel hole is exacting to the nth degree. No tolerances are allowed. When the barrel is fitted to the revolver frame, it must screw up tight and when it is tight, the front sight must be perfectly true on top of the barrel.

Probably no single operation in the assembly of a Colt revolver is gauged and inspected more rigidly and more often than ranging or aligning the chamber bores with the barrel. Before it goes to the shooting gallery, the firearm is ranged. It is ranged again after it is returned, and again in the final inspection. Not only that, but the gauging and the inspection work are rechecked by a second inspection. The perfect alignment of cylinder and barrel of every Colt revolver is a demand, a 'must' and a creed. As some indication of the precision employed in ranging, the maximum wear allowable of the range gauges is .0005 of an inch—or the thickness of a human hair split six times.

Polishing Steel To a Mirror-Like Finish

Some idea of the ultra skill employed in the polishing process may be gleaned from the fact that polishers coming to Colt who have worked elsewhere have to go through a training school. Though experts before, they actually are not good enough to do the fine work that Colt demands. Some of the polishing operations, particularly those involving flat surfaces, are so exacting that 98 out of 100 polishers cannot do the work.

The polishing room is literally a room of wheels—wheels and sparks. These wheels are of all types—flat wheels, form wheels, contour wheels—each designed and suited to a certain polishing operation. The actual polishing of a revolver or an automatic is but a fraction of the total time and cost in-

volved. The preparatory work is enormous—keeping the different polishing wheels in order, resetting them with fresh abrasive, breaking new wheels in—all this is preparatory to the actual polishing of the steel. When you stop to consider that practically every Colt model requires a different set of wheels, you begin to understand what I mean when I say the polishing room is a room of wheels. It is mighty interesting to watch how a polishing wheel is reset. A polishing wheel is made of wood and formed to carefully fit the surface it is going to polish. The rim of the wheel is covered with leather. New leather is given a coating of beef tallow and Japanese wax melted together in secret combinations to gain required texture. Most of the leather is imported: American hides, particularly of late, have not been thick enough to stand the gaff. The leather covered wheels are given a thorough bath and are dipped in hot glue. The rim is then rolled in loose abrasive, the coarseness of which is determined by the job assigned each wheel. The new wheels must then be broken in.

From polishing, we go downstairs to the blueing room.

Moisture is the great enemy of the blueing room. With the care that a hospital operation room fights bacteria, so does the Colt blueing room fight moisture. Nothing is overlooked to constantly guard the surfaces of steel against damaging moisture.

Frames, cylinders, barrels, slides, receivers and parts come to the blueing room direct from the polishing department. Side plates and craned are removed. Everything is first given a bath in hot gasoline… gasoline heated to 150 degrees Fahrenheit. This removes all dirt particles, dust or grease that may have gathered on the way down from the polishing room. Hot air is then forced over them to eliminate all presence of moisture, the arch enemy.

After washing and drying, the side plates (in the case of revolvers) are put back on. But they are put on with 'work screws' that hide beneath the surface so that the entire surface can be completely exposed for cleaning and blueing. When finished, blued screws will replace the work screws.

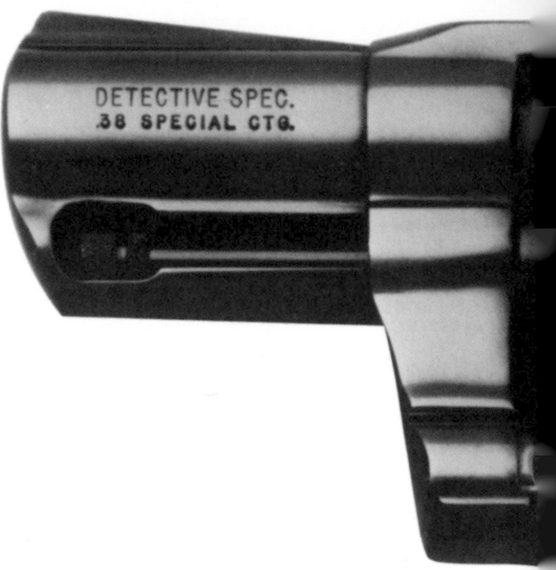

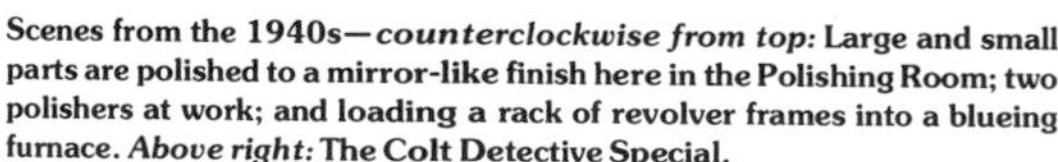

Scenes from the 1940s—*counterclockwise from top:* Large and small parts are polished to a mirror-like finish here in the Polishing Room; two polishers at work; and loading a rack of revolver frames into a blueing furnace. *Above right:* The Colt Detective Special.

All surfaces to be blued are then wiped with a solution of alcohol and whiting—a polishing compound of very fine texture. Wiped with a soft dry cloth, the parts are now chemically clean. From this point on until the blueing process is complete, not a human hand touches a surface to be blued. All this is preparatory to the actual blueing process itself.

A blueing run starts the first thing in the morning. A secret mixture of charred bone and primer is put into the blueing furnaces. The furnaces slowly revolve. Pyrometers control furnace heat. Readings are taken every 15 minutes during the five hours it takes to complete the blueing process, which reaches a high temperature of 650 degrees.

The furnaces are gas fired. Four burners supply the heat in each one, and it is interesting to note that the forward burner is larger to compensate for any heat loss through the doors.

The 'charge' used in the blueing process is ground animal bone charred to chemical purity in a bone pot placed into a white hot furnace at 1400 degrees. Two hundred pounds of bone are charred at a time, burning away all foreign matter.

The 'primer' is bone, soaked in pure petroleum oil. Even the oil is boiled to remove moisture and foreign matter: it must be chemically pure. The primer is what gives off the smoke that keeps free oxygen away from the pieces being blued in the revolving drums. The 'primer' and 'charge' are mixed and put into the furnace before the work goes in.

What is the chemistry of blueing anyway? How does this blueing process impart the handsome and lasting blued steel finish so famous in modern firearms? Blueing is a combination of carbonizing and oxidizing, which, with heat brings the inherent carbon of the steel through the open pores to the surface: all the coloring is done by heat. No particle of bone ever touches the parts being blued—the smoke given off by the 'primer' expels free oxygen from the drum, leaving only sufficient oxygen to allow combustion. The primer and the charge control the composition of gas in the furnace; the heavy carbon dioxide shielding the parts from contact with oxygen. All this calls for expert knowledge and experience in mixing the proper proportions of the primer and charge—not only to obtain the proper color, but to create a smoke that is free from moisture. Otherwise—though blued, the pieces would be pitted.

When you buy a Colt revolver or automatic with full blued finish, a full blued finish is what you get. Even the inside of your barrel is blued. And there is something beautiful about blued steel that even an artist of words could hardly describe.

Over a hundred fabricating hammers a week are used in manufacturing Colt revolvers and automatic pistols. You must wonder how hammers could wear out so quickly. But these are not ordinary hammers. They are lead hammers and are used because lead is softer than steel and therefore can do it no harm. In filing, fitting and assembling it is often necessary to slightly tap the frame with a hammer in order to loosen a side plate or a crane fitting that fits too tightly—for which lead hammers are used. Incidentally, they are made right in the Colt factory—thousands of them. Using lead hammers is just another way with which Colt 'Care-On-Little-Things' is expressed.

All the parts that go into the manufacture of a Colt revolver or automatic—even the incidental ones like the stocks, the springs, screws and etc—are made right in the Colt plant.

There is a well equipped woodworking shop in which the grips are turned out. Colt grips are made from selected walnut. The actual shaping of a pair of Colt grips is pretty much a matter of conventional wood turning. Finishing them, however, is a horse of another color (no Colt pun intended). The filing, sandpapering and hand finishing require patience that only those who are satisfied with nothing less than best possess. Perhaps the most outstanding machine in this department is the checkering machine. I was thrilled watching this ingenious automatic machine that, with mathematical precision, cuts the tiny but deep grooves that result in checkered grips. Shooters all agree that beautifully deep checkered stocks add security to the grip... essential to firing line confidence.

The proper and dependable action of the firing mechanism's springs constitutes an important function in the operation of a firearm. In the automatic, of course, there are the main spring, the recoil spring and the firing pin spring. Springs in a revolver include the bolt spring, latch spring and ejector rod spring. You might naturally think that

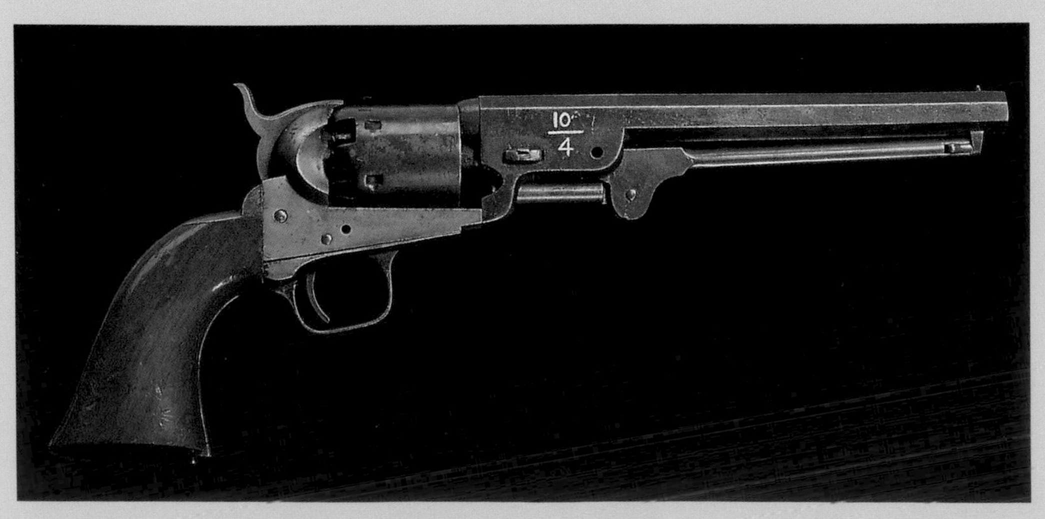
10
4

Top: A presentation-grade Improved Old Model Army, circa 1858-1861. *Above:* A presentation-grade variation on the 1862 Pocket Pistol. *At left:* A .36 caliber Colt Navy revolver, with plain blued finish.

Above: **Hand checkering pistol stocks in the mid-20th century.** ***Below:*** **Note the tools that this assembler used to fit and adjust parts into a finished pistol.** ***At right:*** **John Wayne and Joanna Barnes look on as Kirk Douglas extols his Peacemaker in the movie** ***The War Wagon.***

the Colt company would purchase its springs, but they do not—they make them themselves. The quality of springs that Colt demands is not obtainable anywhere in the country. Years ago Colt's engineers designed and built machines to make springs to the specifications desired. Occasional efforts have been made since that time to determine whether the same specifications could not be met outside the plant, but to date no manufacturer of springs can be found who will meet Colt demands.

First of all, triple A wire is used. The dimensions of the wire must be exact, the number of coils to a given length must be exact, the wright must be exact, and all these specifications must tally after the springs are heat treated to specified temper. A spring is ordinarily just a few coils of wire, but with Colt it is a major part to be fussed over until it's exactly right and unvaryingly efficient.

When the gun has been built, assembled and tested, only one more thing is necessary and then the gun is ready to go to the shipping room as a full fledged Colt. That one thing is inspection—inspection with a capital 'I.' From the shooting gallery, their testor-signed targets accompanying them, Colt firearms go to the inspection room where a veteran of long

Colt "Service Model Ace" Automatic Pistol

CALIBER:
.22 Long Rifle
(Both Regular and High Speed Ammunition)

WITH FLOATING CHAMBER

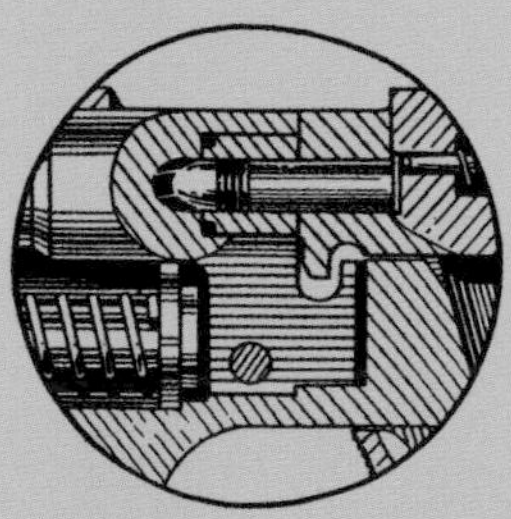

New Floating Chamber Increases Recoil Approximately Four Times

A feature of the Service Ace is its ingenious "floating chamber" which amplifies the ordinary recoil of a .22 four times, and provides positive functioning under all conditions.
The floating chamber is a marvel of simplicity . . . consisting of a movable chamber, so designed as to increase pressure, building up the recoil until it simulates the recoil of the .45 caliber automatic pistol. The Service ACE is a natural for military shooters, a remarkably fine training gun for beginners.

Specifications

CAPACITY OF MAGAZINE: 10 cartridges.

LENGTH OF BARREL: 5 inches.

LENGTH OVER ALL: 8½ inches.

ACTION: Hand finished.

WEIGHT: 42 ounces.

STOCKS: Checked Walnut.

TRIGGER AND HAMMER SPUR: Checked.

FINISH: Full Blued.

SIGHTS: Ramp front sight, fixed. Rear sight adjustable for both elevation and windage. Both stippled.

ARCHED HOUSING:Checked.

The New Service Model Ace has been designed to provide efficient and economical target practice for military men, and all shooters of the heavy frame Colt Automatic Pistols. It is similar in design to the regular Ace Model . . . plus the recently perfected Floating Chamber. By the use of the Floating Chamber the recoil has been increased four times, simulating the recoil found in the .45 caliber Government Model Automatic Pistol. Thus the shooter is trained with an arm that allows him to later change to the heavier caliber pistol, without the additional recoil being noticeable. Because of the much lower cost of .22 caliber ammunition the Service Ace will pay for itself in a very short time.

Special Features

Except for difference in caliber, the new SERVICE MODEL ACE and the Government Model .45 are practically twins. They are so near alike that you can switch from one to the other and hardly notice the difference. However, the Service Ace is provided with hand finished action and a two-way Stevens adjustable rear sight. The front sight is fixed with serrated face.

The Service Ace saves *real* money and pays for itself in a very short time. It provides accurate, economical target shooting for Service men — members of National Guard, Reserve Officers, and individual shooters of the .45 Caliber Automatic Pistol . . . at one-seventh the cost of .45 automatic cartridges.

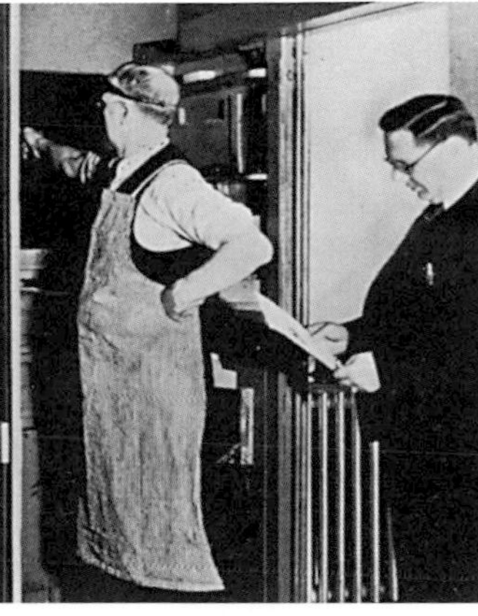

Colt .45-.22 "Conversion Unit"

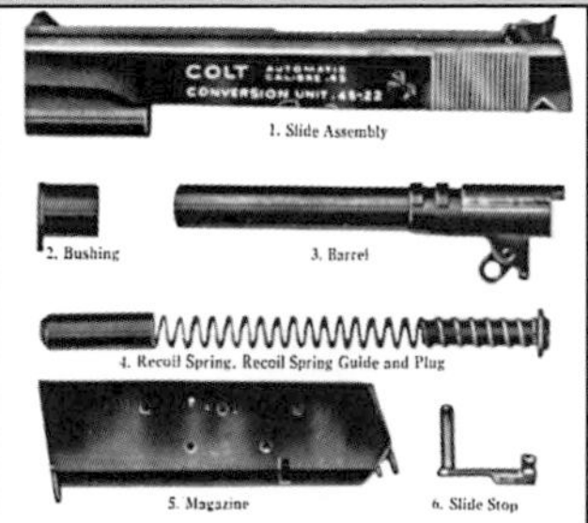

For Converting the Colt Service Model Ace .22 to a .45 Caliber Pistol

The New .45-.22 Conversion Unit converts the recently developed .22 caliber Service Ace (with Floating Chamber) to caliber .45. By simply interchanging the component parts of the Unit with the corresponding parts of the Service Ace, the shooter may shift from .22 caliber ammunition to .45 Automatic cartridges in a very few minutes. The .45-.22 is composed of Match Grade slide, equipped with fixed front sight and either fixed or Stevens adjustable rear sight; selected Match barrel with bushing; recoil spring, recoil spring guide and plug; magazine and slide stop. This new Unit makes it possible for you to secure maximum pleasure from your Colt Service Ace.

years goes over them 'with a fine-toothed comb.' He looks them over thoroughly, gauges certain fittings, ranges them again, checks action and trigger pull, and literally mothers them like they were lost orphans. If they pass final inspection and 9/10ths of them will, they are put into stock in the shipping room, wrapped in soft tissue and boxed. A Colt has to earn its VP—the 'Verified Proof' mark. This is truly a badge of perfection which the final inspectors strike on to the metal after they have given a firearm a 'clean bill of health' to go out into the world and uphold the Colt reputation for building the world's finest hand guns. But a Colt has to earn it—it must pass every test, every inspection by a good margin or else the VP does not go on. The VP mark is held in high honor by Colt workmen. They know, better than anyone else, that when a firearm finally gets its VP it is a true Colt—a thoroughbred.

The thing that impressed me perhaps more than any other single thing in my whole trip through the mammoth Colt plant is the absolute and utter care given to the manufacture of a Colt revolver or automatic pistol. I have seen precision manufacturing before. But never, never have I seen so many—and so minute—gaugings, inspections, re-gaugings and tests put into the manufacture of a single product.

Not only is meticulous care given to each machine operation, but the deliberate and unhurried hand fittings, the skilled benchwork, is of a character that one might easily and truthfully associate with only the great guilds of medieval craftsmen. Craftsmanship, skill and practical knowledge born only of experience is the important human tool that builds a Colt revolver. Gauges catch any faulty mechanical operation, but the human eye, the human hand and long years of experience are the factors that account for the unchallenged accuracy, the smoothness of operation and the absolute dependability of a Colt.

In my desire to emphasize the skill of the old school I must not give you the impression that the Colt factory is run by old men—by no means: rubbing elbows with these older gentlemen are youthful, keen-eyed, stalwart young men ambitious to carry on the spirit and traditions of each of their crafts. On my travels through the Colt factory, occasionally losing my own bearings in their 50-odd acres of floor space, I made it a particular observation to note in my mind how the problem of developing apprentices was being met. I was deeply impressed with the type of young men serving the plant and the seriousness with which they accept the responsibility of their separate functions. Craftsmanship is in their blood.

***Opposite and above:* Ads from Colt's 1940 catalogue. *Left:* Checking a revolver in Colt's Final Inspection Room. *Above left:* Testing Officers' Models in the Shooting Gallery. *Overleaf:* In the Old West, you always had to be prepared—John Wayne and Kirk Douglas test their Colts in one of the many films in which Mr Wayne and Mr Douglas starred.**

Excellence

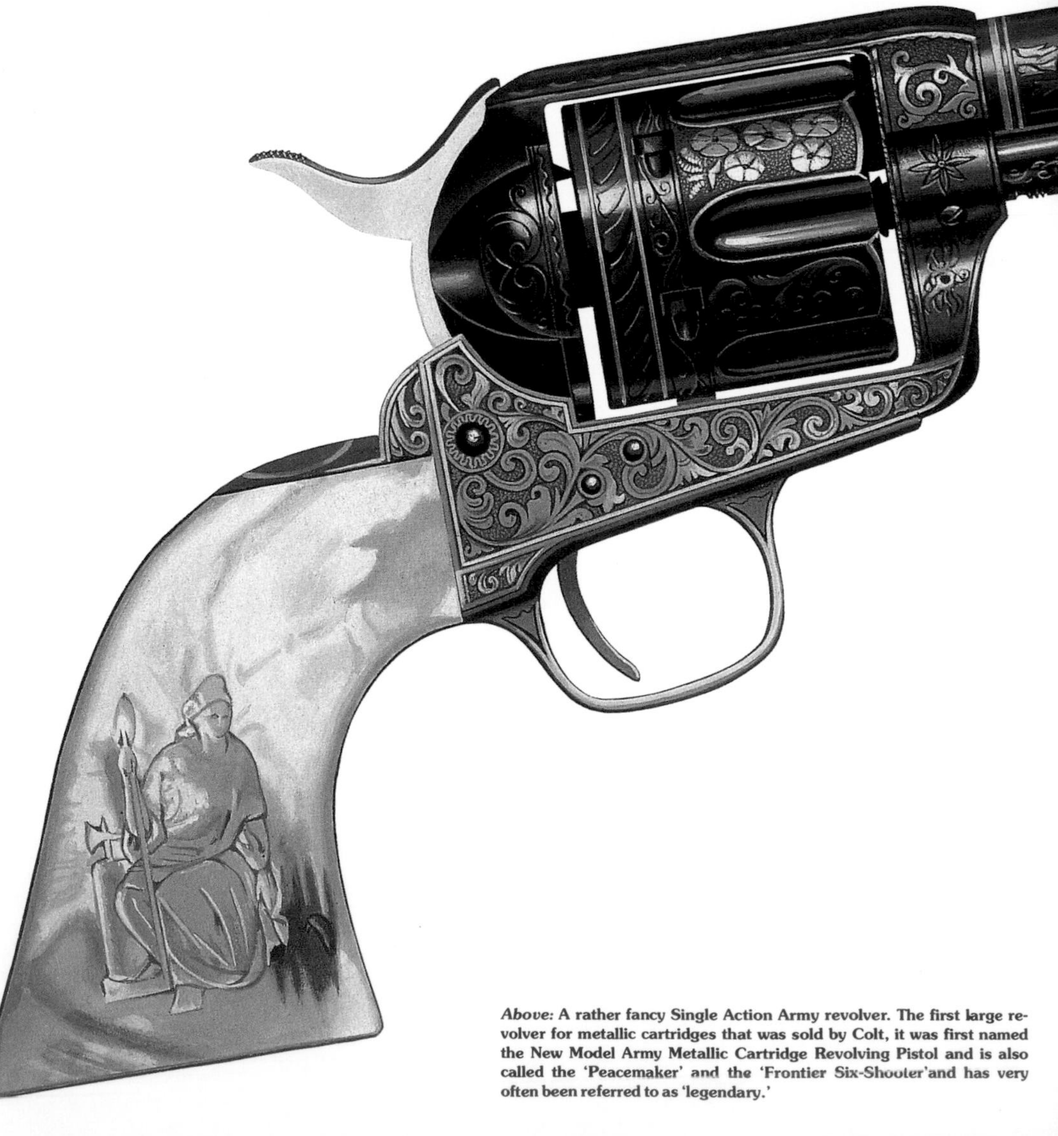

Above: **A rather fancy Single Action Army revolver. The first large revolver for metallic cartridges that was sold by Colt, it was first named the New Model Army Metallic Cartridge Revolving Pistol and is also called the 'Peacemaker' and the 'Frontier Six-Shooter'and has very often been referred to as 'legendary.'**

and Art

In the realm of firearms hand engraving, the words 'custom' and 'factory' have similar but distinctive meanings. Custom engraving is the product of a special and specific request by the client to decorate a gun with certain selected patterns and, in some cases, the use of precious metals. Factory engraving is done in more traditional and standardized styles of engraving. Journeymen engravers work on this type of project, whereas the master engravers are assigned the custom work.

Pricing for engraving is generally made on the basis of how much of the firearm is covered with the artwork. Letters of the alphabet denominate this coverage factor. 'A' is one-quarter coverage, 'B' is one-half coverage, 'C' is three-quarters coverage, and 'D' is full coverage.

The Colt Custom Gun Shop performs special services to enhance most Colt products cosmetically and functionally. The time-honored Colt Single Action Army revolver is produced and sold in limited quantities exclusively by the Colt Custom Shop, for sale to collectors of fine firearms. The Custom Shop produced several unique Single Action variations for 1986. These models used the old style black-powder frame design that featured a base pin screw, a round ejector rod head, a three-line patent date rollmark on the frame, an Italic rollmark on the barrel and caliber stamp under the barrel on the .44-40 caliber model.

Colt offers its custom services on all current firearms featured in the standard commercial products catalog, and will consider work on older Colt models—on a case-by-case basis (depending upon availability of replacement parts).

The Custom Gun Shop has historically supplied collectors of fine art with hand engraved firearms of premium quality. Production firearms are enhanced through the time-honored craft of embellishing metal, utilizing the hands of Colt's world-renowned master engravers. Colt engravers handcarve traditional engraving patterns, and inlay both flush and raised reliefs with precious metals to enhance the appearance and worth of firearms submitted to their care. The engravers provide five different scroll patterns: Classic American, (and, upon special request) Oakleaf, Vine, English or Nimschke styles of engraving. Colt master engraving provides the finest balance and detail available today. In addition, each piece is individually signed by the master engraver—and this has historically contributed to greater desirability and value. Additionally, master-engraved firearms can be documented in detail on Colt letterhead by the Colt Historian.

Custom engraving pricing is based on the amount of coverage desired, complexity of style and time required for special requests. The engraving pattern will be designed and quoted by experienced Custom Shop personnel, who can offer the collector valuable insight into the design of a personalized firearm. These truly unique Colts can currently be created in less than a year.

The Custom Shop offers hand engraving performed by journeyman engravers that complements any Colt firearm. Engraving may be special ordered to highlight individual parts of the firearm. The four basic decoration areas of the Single Action Army are the barrel, the cylinder, the frame and the trigger guard/backstrap. Colt hand engraving designs, based on a variation of the American style, are chosen by the engraver. Coverage on other Colt models is consistent with their four traditional coverages, unless a specific quotation is requested. The Colt Custom Gun Shop can deliver these types of orders currently in less than six months.

The Custom Gun Shop accepts requests for limited production (minimum of 50 firearms) Colt firearms. This is ideal for organizations who wish to incorporate mottos, dates and pictures into artwork of their customized firearm. Anniversary, celebration and fund raiser commemorative edition firearms for fraternal, civic, military and law enforcement groups have been successfully created by Colt. The Custom Shop selectively plates guns in gold or silver with the finest detail offered in the industry today, and can hand

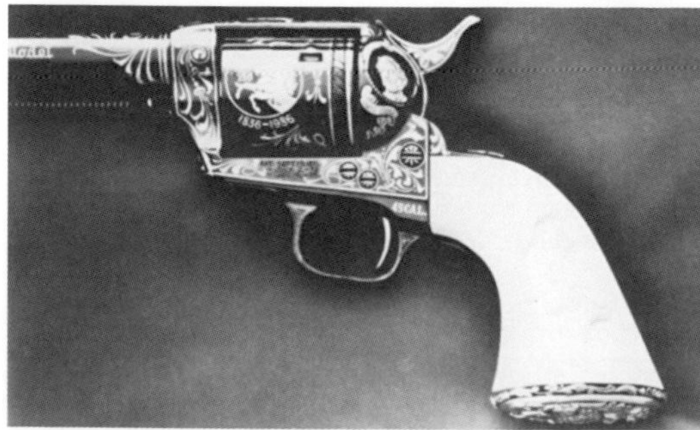

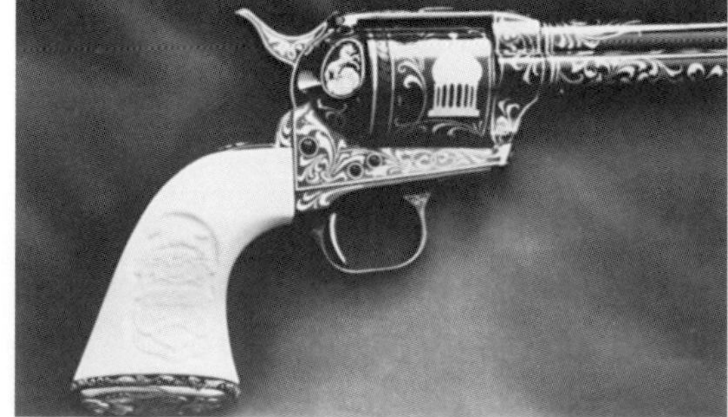

Opposite: Colt's 150th Anniversary Exhibition Gun, based on the 'Peacemaker' of Wild West fame. Grip engravings feature the young Sam Colt whittling the prototype from which the modern revolver would evolve, a head portrait of Colt on the receiver flange, Colt's 'rampant colt' logo on the cylinder, and portraits of the Python Ultimate revolver and Officer's ACP on the barrel. *Top:* The grips butt of the 150th Anniversary Gun. *Above left and right:* A 'flip side' view of its receiver with engravings.

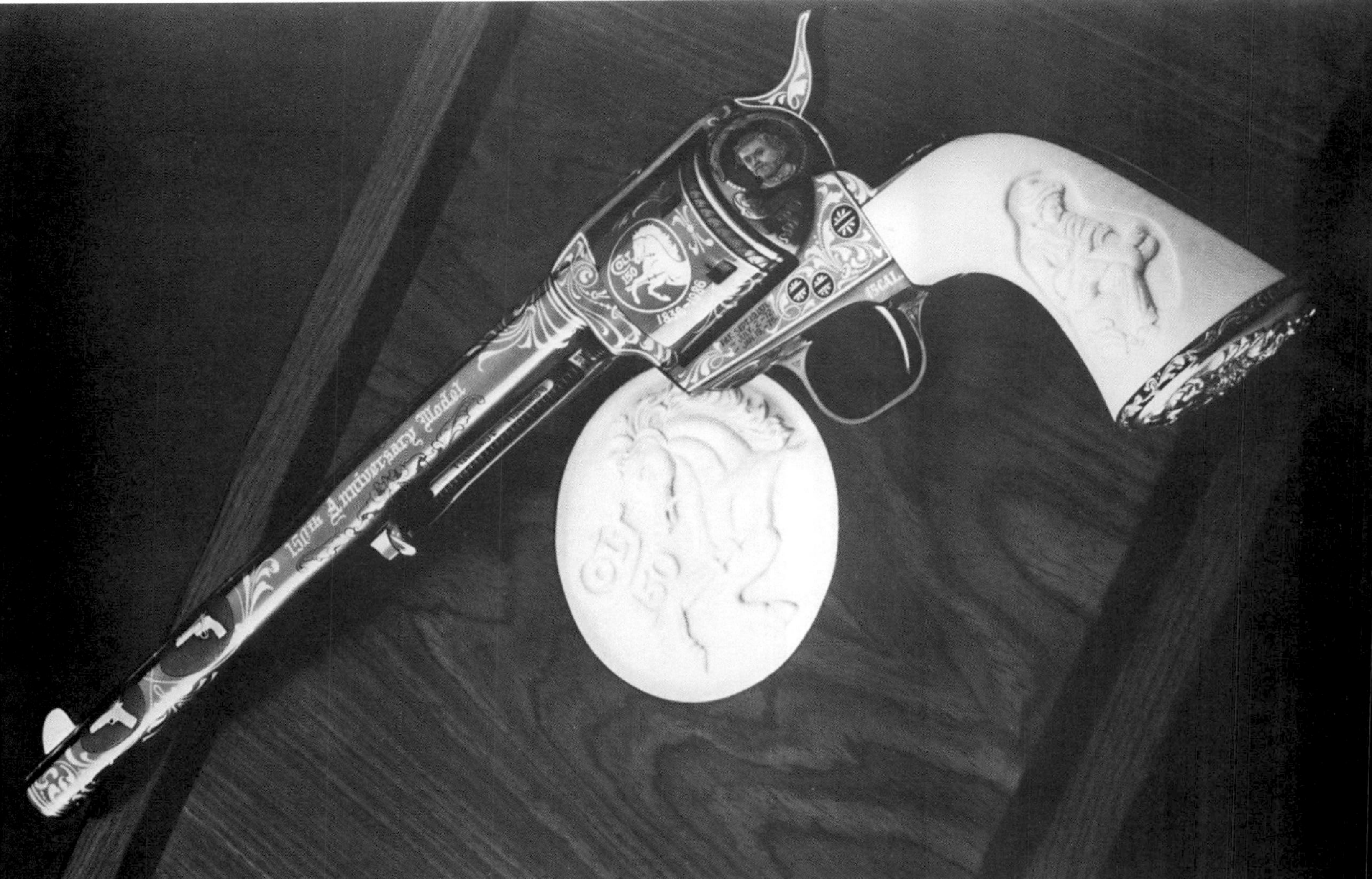
150th Anniversary Model
1836-1986

***Above left and right:* Samples from the Colt Custom Shop—inlays, motifs and scroll styles. *Below:* An ad for Colt ornamentation in 1940. *Opposite:* A historical letter from the Colt Historian, tracing the history of a collector's Colt by means of factory records.**

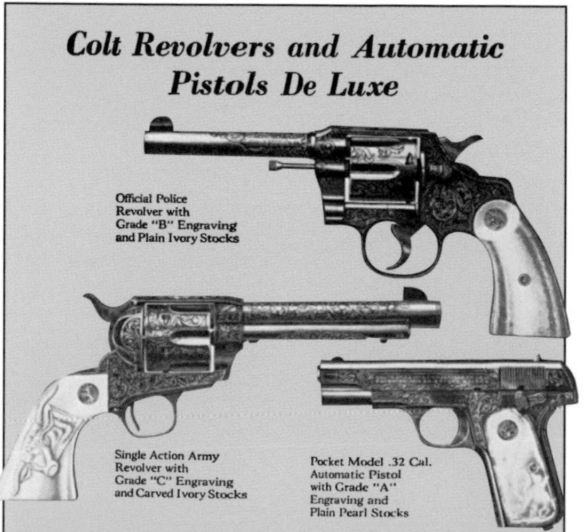

Colt Revolvers and Automatic Pistols De Luxe

Official Police Revolver with Grade "B" Engraving and Plain Ivory Stocks

Single Action Army Revolver with Grade "C" Engraving and Carved Ivory Stocks

Pocket Model .32 Cal. Automatic Pistol with Grade "A" Engraving and Plain Pearl Stocks

Whether for presentation purposes, as special match prizes or the favorite Arm of a shooter, Colts may be had in almost any special finish or decoration desired. We have always taken special pride and given the greatest attention to such ornamented Arms. A Colt of any model (except .22 Automatic Pistol) may be fitted with select stocks in choice Pearl or Ivory (either carved or plain). All genuine Colt Pearl or Ivory stocks are identified by the rampant Colt medallion. Special price list of Fancy Stocks, sent upon request.

Engraving may be had in any one of the three grades illustrated in the models shown above. The grade refers only to the amount of engraving desired, "A" representing the minimum, "B" medium grade and "C" the most ornamental. The quality of work is the same in all cases and performed by the same experts.

Also we can furnish Colt Arms with any special design desired, with full gold or silver plating or inlaid State or National seals, etc., also Pearl or Ivory Stocks with inlaid enamel initials or emblems in colors. The work in this department is performed by highly skilled craftsmen only, who have had years of experience in this painstaking and beautiful designing. Estimates for all work of this character are furnished in advance.

engrave to the specifications of individuals or organizations, polish to presentation grade cosmetic standards and fit guns with unique stocks and stock decorations. Customers may design cosmetic or functional features to create a unique variation on current Colt model offerings and the Custom Shop will fabricate their designs. Unique presentation packaging can be ordered to complement and protect the 'customized' firearms.

The Custom Shop polishers have prided themselves on attention to detail and the quality of finish that is evident in Colt Royal Blue and special plated firearms. The 'Mirror Brite' finish imparts an ultra buffed sheen to all exterior parts of the firearm. Great attention is paid to highlighting surfaces, which results in firearms of high polishing standards.

Colt firearms may be refinished in blue, blue and color case, Colt Guard, Royal Blue and nickel. Prices will vary depending on the model and condition of firearms. All modern firearms returned for refinishing are cleaned, given minor adjustments and test fired.

The Custom Gun Shop can enhance the presentation of any Colt firearm with a select wood presentation case. These fine cases, crafted from oak, cherry or walnut are available with 'French fit'—partitioned interiors of rich velvet. Custom etched or engraved plates may be ordered to further enrich the presentation of guns produced for special awards, retirements, anniversaries or birthdays. All custom

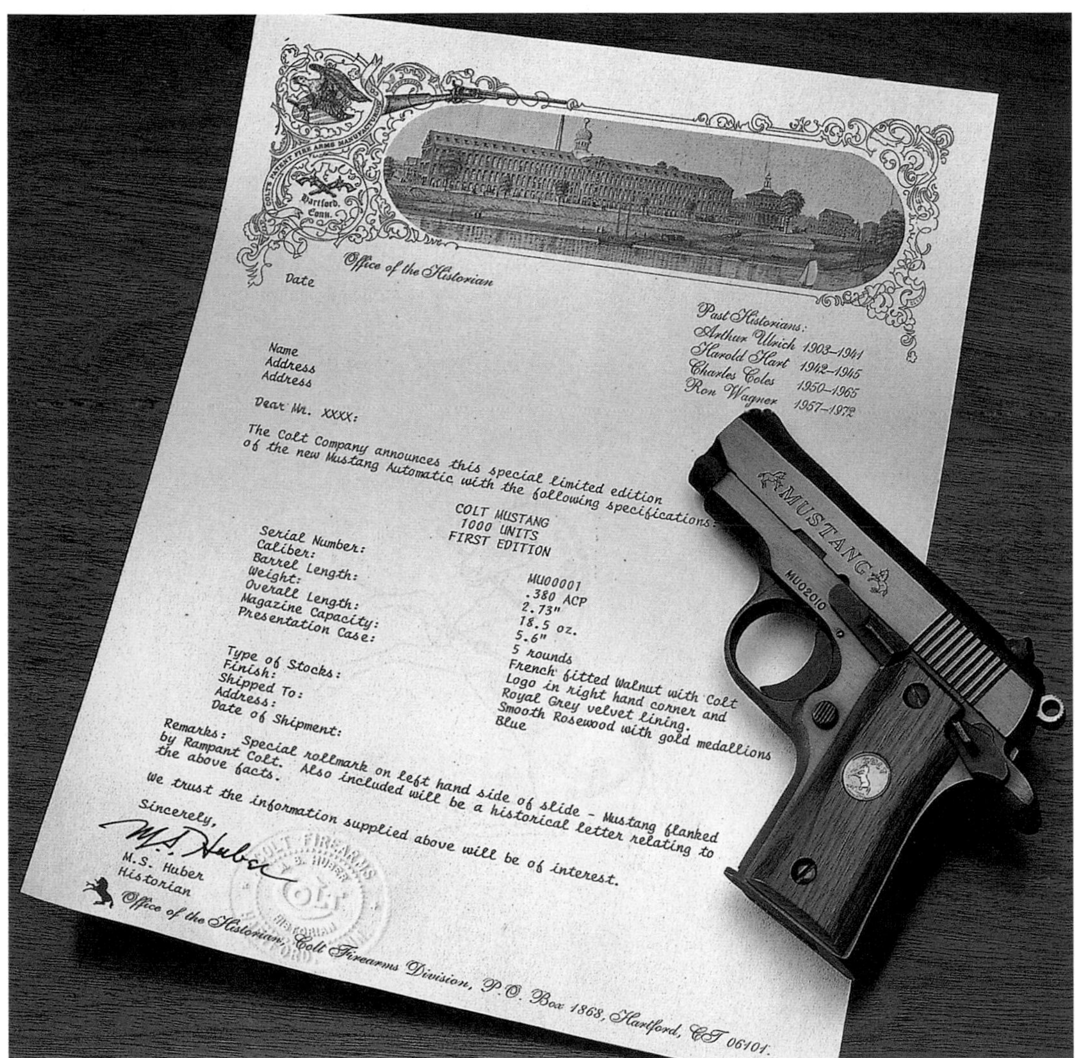

Office of the Historian

Date

Past Historians:
Arthur Ulrich 1903–1941
Harold Hart 1942–1945
Charles Coles 1950–1965
Ron Wagner 1957–1972

Name
Address
Address

Dear Mr. XXXX:

The Colt Company announces this special limited edition of the new Mustang Automatic with the following specifications:

COLT MUSTANG
1000 UNITS
FIRST EDITION

Serial Number:	MU00001
Caliber:	.380 ACP
Barrel Length:	2.73"
Weight:	18.5 oz.
Overall Length:	5.6"
Magazine Capacity:	5 rounds
Presentation Case:	French fitted Walnut with Colt Logo in right hand corner and Royal Grey velvet lining.
Type of Stocks:	Smooth Rosewood with gold medallions
Finish:	Blue
Shipped To:	
Address:	
Date of Shipment:	

Remarks: Special rollmark on left hand side of slide - Mustang flanked by Rampant Colt. Also included will be a historical letter relating to the above facts.

We trust the information supplied above will be of interest.

Sincerely,

M.S. Huber
M.S. Huber
Historian

Office of the Historian, Colt Firearms Division, P.O. Box 1868, Hartford, CT 06101.

cases are manufactured to the highest quality standards to ensure compatibility with the firearms and the setting in which they will be displayed. A choice of blue, red or forest green lining colors are available.

A new line of glass wall/walnut frame presentation cases is available that allows an upright firearm to be viewed from four sides and top while protecting the firearm from the adverse effects of unsupervised handling. These cases are ideal for collector shows and are available on special order for most current models.

The Custom Gun Shop also presents fine, crafted custom grips: grips of ivory, and of rosewood, walnut and bacote woods can be fitted to all Colt models. Grips can be ordered with gold or nickel Rampant Colt medallions to complement the color of the finish selected on the firearm. Colt Single Action Army grips are now crafted with a blind screw hole on the left grip to enhance their appearance. Single Action Army wood grips can now be custom fitted to the traditional one piece configuration upon request. Checkered grips in the fleur-de-lis pattern can be ordered for the Single Action Army in any of the above choices of grip material. Special grip medallions may also be ordered on commissioned products.

The Colt Historian authenticates production and shipping information essential to establishing the value of firearms. A Colt historical letter adds value to any collection piece by adding knowledge about past or current production. Letters serve to assure buyers and sellers that the basic physical characteristics of a gun are consistent with original factory records. Letters also provide valuable documentation for insurance policies that must rely on appraisals and certifications of authenticity. Thus the investor, the history buff and the collector all derive valuable benefits from this unique service.

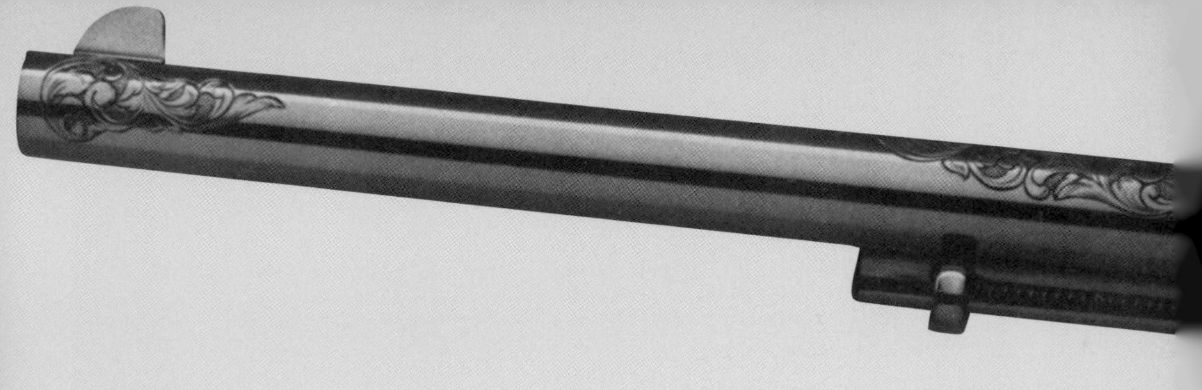

At left: What more could a Wild West enthusiast want? This hobbyist seems pleased with his collection of Log Cabin Library magazines and his beautifully engraved Colt. *Above top and bottom:* A fine-grade Colt 150th Anniversary Commemorative pistol and a Colt 150th Anniversary Engraving Sampler in four styles of engraving.

PAT. SEPT.19.1871.
" JULY. 2.—72.
" JAN.19.—75.
PAT. SEPT.19.1871.
" JULY. 2.—72.
" JAN.19.—75.
R. Henshaw 1831
L. Nimschke 1850-19
C. Helfricht 1871-192
Contemporary

The Traditior

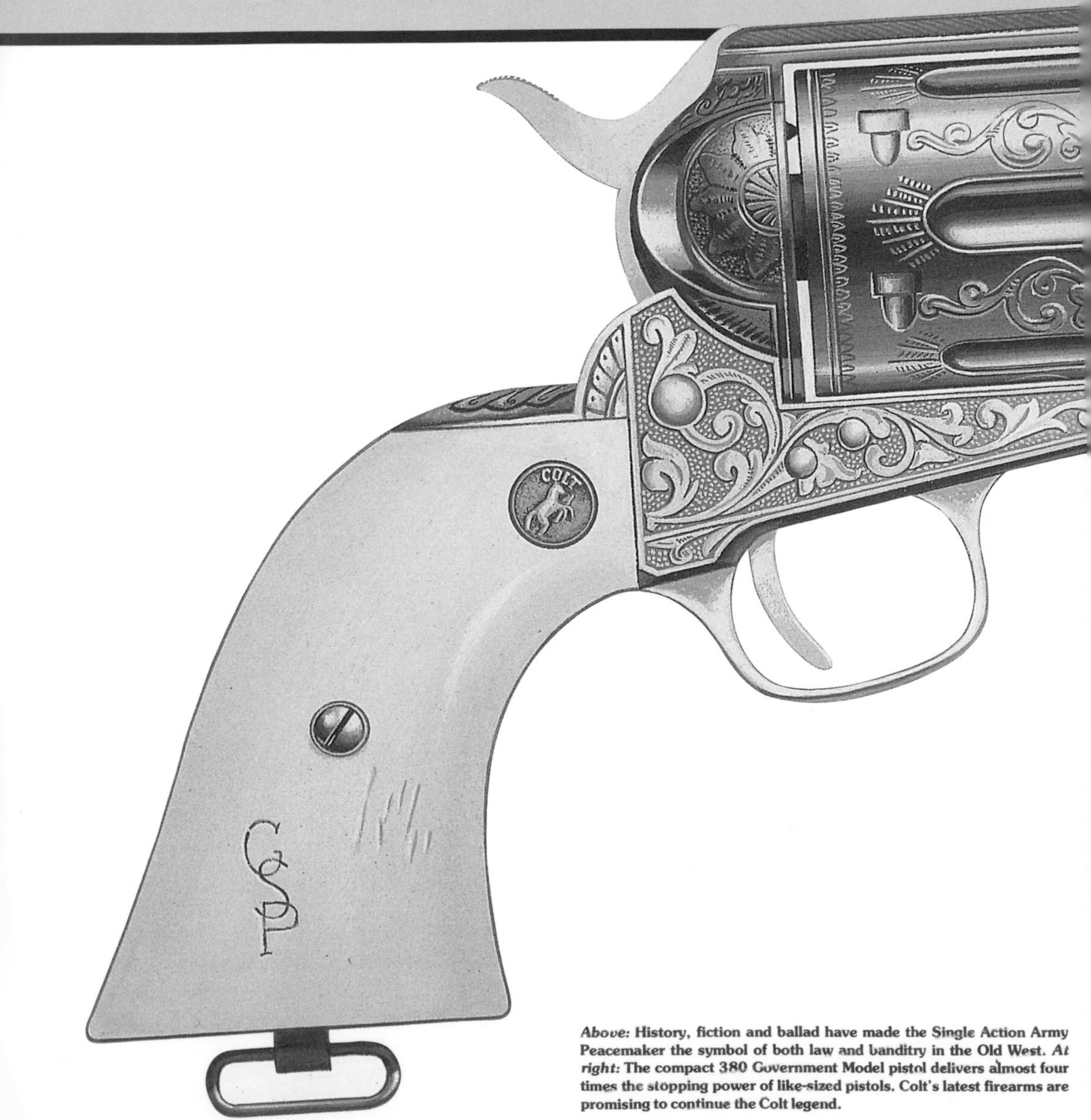

Above: History, fiction and ballad have made the Single Action Army Peacemaker the symbol of both law and banditry in the Old West. *At right:* The compact 380 Government Model pistol delivers almost four times the stopping power of like-sized pistols. Colt's latest firearms are promising to continue the Colt legend.

Continues

Today the tradition of excellence continues on at Colt. Bill Stokes, Vice President of Manufacturing says, 'The bottom line is to build the quality into Colt products at the very beginning rather than repairing them over a period of time.'

Colt employs extensive quality improvement programs in all phases of production and finishing. These programs require supervisors to inspect the production outputs of their respective departments at least twice per day. These inspections are made using gauges, micrometers and other testing apparatus. When a new run of parts is begun, this inspection process is actually a careful observation of *all* parts on that run as opposed to a random sampling.

Those particular parts of a firearm that could affect function and safety are denominated 'critical operations' and extra attention is paid to their fabrication and milling.

Every setup person and supervisor is required by Colt to attend a 22 week training program at Hartford State Technical Institute. The 88 hours of classroom work is taken up with such subjects as reading a blue print, setting up a particular machine properly, and the basic shop math needed to carry out assigned responsibilities.

Colt personnel are also trained in the use of computer aided design and manufacturing processes. Colt is in the midst of a modernization program which will bring these technologies to bear upon its products.

Since the raw materials used in the fabrication of the firearm are just as important as the finished product, Colt's quality control extends 'backwards' to their supplier's operations, as well. Each year, Colt Firearms gives its 'Vendor of the Year Award' to its best supplier on the basis of quality and dependability of delivery.

But quality control does not begin with the raw material and end with the finished product for Colt. Colt Firearms maintains a customer service center as well as 120 local service centers worldwide. Even this service center network is currently being computerized in order to ensure ongoing customer satisfaction.

The history of Colt firearms began with cap and ball pistols and moved through the conversion processes involved in adapting to the new center-fire cartridges. Single action, and then double action revolvers were, and still are, produced. The turn of the century brought the advent of automatic weapons to the Colt line of products. Today, Colt firearms defend the nation as a whole, and its citizenry in particular. The spirit of Samuel Colt lives on.

At top: **Colt's Double Diamond .357 Magnum revolver with vent-rib barrel, adjustable sights, polished finish and fine wooden grips.** ***Above:*** **Colt's compact, sophisticated Double Diamond 45 Automatic.**

GLOSSARY OF TERMS

Action. Generally defined as the moving parts of a firearm. Three basic 'actions' are prevalent in the world of small firearms. These are: single action, double action and automatic (semi and full).

Anvil. The actual piece of metal in the primer of a centerfire metallic cartridge which comes into direct contact with the priming compound at the blow of the hammer.

Ball. *(see Bullet)*

Barrel. The tube through which the bullet is propelled by the powder explosion. The 'bore' of a barrel is its inside diameter. The 'muzzle' of a barrel is the end furthest from the user. The 'breech' of a barrel is the end nearest the user.

Barrel Key. Sometimes called the 'barrel bolt.' A key which holds the barrel to the center pin of the frame.

Barrel Lug. A block of metal forming the frame of percussion-cap Colt revolvers which was threaded to hold the jointed-lever ramrod in place.

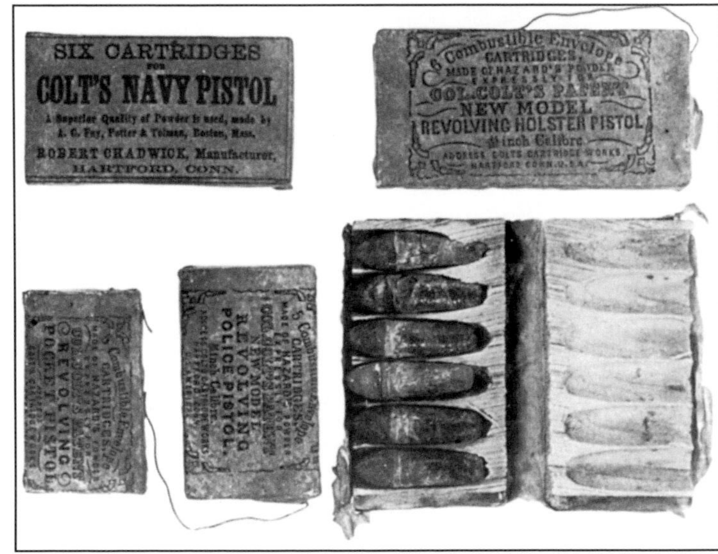

Bore. *(see Barrel)*

Breech. *(see Barrel)*

Bullet. The projectile fired from cartridge firearms. 'Balls' are bullets which are fired from early firearms. 'Shot' is generally thought of as being a collection of bullets or balls fired from the same enclosure.

Butt. Usually the shoulder rest of the wooden stock of a firearm.

Carbine. A shortened rifle.

Cartridge. Technically the housing for the powder or explosive charge, but generally defined as the housing, the charge and projectile together.

Center Fire. A metallic cartridge fired by a primer located in the center of the rear of the shell.

Center Pin. The pin on which the cylinder revolves. At one time referred to as the 'arbor.'

Chamfer. A bevel in the barrel of a percussion cap revolver used to make it easier to load the bullet into the chamber.

Chamber. The bored recessions in the cylinder of a revolver meant to hold the charges.

Cock. An early name for the hammer of a revolver.

Cylinder. The round revolving breech piece bored with chambers which holds the cap, powder and ball or, depending on the modernity of the firearm, the cartridge, of a revolver.

***Clockwise from immediate left:* A Mustang 380, well suited as a law enforcement backup gun; Colt-armed security police at Beale AFB; combustible envelope cartridges made for use in Colt's percussion cap revolving pistols—the type shown here were made under a patent taken out in 1862. *Above:* US troops on patrol with M16s and M60 light machine guns, both of which have been standard issue since the Vietnam War.**

Cylinder-locking Bolt. The bolt which locks the cylinder in such a manner that one of the chambers is always in line with the barrel.

Deringer. A small single-shot pistol made by Henry Deringer of Philadelphia, Pennsylvania. It has come to define all very small pistols usually used for personal protection.

Double Action. A revolver action in which the pulling of the trigger both cocks the hammer and turns the cylinder as well as fires the cartridge.

Ejector. The device for removing the cartridge case from the firearm after it has been fired.

Firing Pin. A small pin in the frame of a firearm that, when struck by the hammer, comes into direct contact with the cartridge and fires it.

Forestock. That part of the wood stock of certain firearms which lies in front of the trigger.

Fulminate Of Mercury. A chemical compound of mercury which explodes when struck by a sharp blow.

Grip or Grips. The usually wood or rubber hold for the hand, by which pistols are held.

Hammer. The hammerlike piece of metal which is released by the action of the trigger and strikes either a firing pin, or directly strikes the primer of the cartridge, thus discharging the load in the firearm's chamber.

Hammer Spring. The spring which provides the energy for the driving force of the hammer. Sometimes called a 'mainspring.'

Loading Gate or **Loading Notch.** In certain cartridge revolvers, this was the opening through which cartridges were put in, and removed from, the cylinder.

Lock. In early literature, the 'lock' can be substituted for our modern word, 'action.'

Matchlock. This was the first type of mechanical ignition system used in a firearm.

Maynard's Tape Primers. An invention in the 1850s which was much like children's caps today. A roll of these primers was inserted into the magazine of a percussion cap pistol and were fed into proximity with powder in the cylinder by the act of cocking the hammer prior to discharge.

Musket. The first kind of shoulder arm widely used by infantry soldiers. Muskets first came into prominence in the 16th and 17th centuries. The standard musket of the 18th and early 19th centuries was .69 caliber smoothbore.

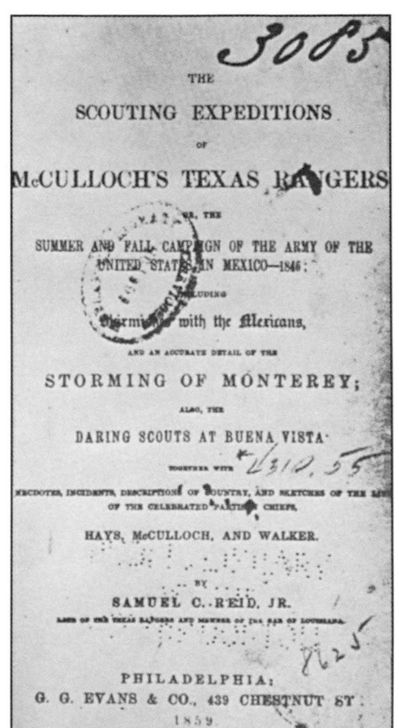

THE
SCOUTING EXPEDITIONS
OF
McCULLOCH'S TEXAS RANGERS
OR, THE
SUMMER AND FALL CAMPAIGN OF THE ARMY OF THE UNITED STATES IN MEXICO—1846;
INCLUDING
Skirmishes with the Mexicans,
AND AN ACCURATE DETAIL OF THE
STORMING OF MONTEREY;
ALSO, THE
DARING SCOUTS AT BUENA VISTA
TOGETHER WITH
ANECDOTES, INCIDENTS, DESCRIPTIONS OF COUNTRY, AND SKETCHES OF THE LIVES OF THE CELEBRATED PARTISAN CHIEFS,
HAYS, McCULLOCH, AND WALKER.
BY
SAMUEL C. REID, JR.
LATE OF THE TEXAS RANGERS AND MEMBER OF THE BAR OF LOUISIANA.
PHILADELPHIA:
G. G. EVANS & CO., 439 CHESTNUT ST.
1859.

Nipple. A small protrusion on each chamber of a percussion cap arm upon which the percussion cap is placed.

Pepperbox. A particular kind of cap and ball revolver that involved the turning of a single, large cylinder in which each chamber also formed its own individual barrel.

Percussion Cap. A small copper container open at one end containing a small amount of fulminate of mercury. The cap is placed over the nipple of the cylinder of a cap and ball firearm and provides the ignition charge for the powder when struck by the hammer.

Pistol. A firearm intended for use in one hand only.

Primer. A form of percussion cap mounted into the body of a center fire cartridge.

Ramrod. In old muzzle-loading arms, this was the wood or metal piece used for running the charge down the barrel.

At left: **American generals who toted Colt pistols in WWII: Generals Eisenhower, Patton, Bradley and Hodges.** ***Above:*** **The Texas Rangers often rely on Colts.** ***At right:*** **General Curtis LeMay, proponent of the M16.** ***Overleaf:*** **Colts helped to decide the Civil War.**

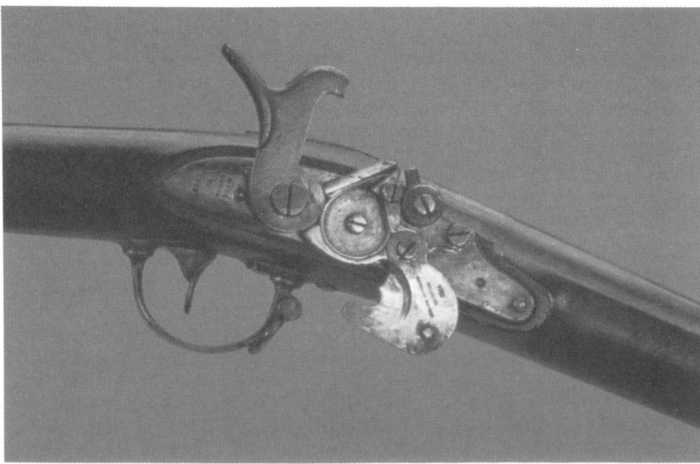

This page, clockwise from above: **Detail of the Maynard Tape Priming system; A Colt Heirloom 1 'mirror brite' .45 caliber Officer's ACP; and hand tuning Colt revolvers and pistol actions.** ***Immediate opposite:*** **A US soldier samples his tasty rations with his M16 nearby.** ***Above opposite:*** **American students greet US troops in Grenada.** ***Far right:*** **Colt's new Delta auto pistol and Delta Heavy Barrel (H-Bar) AR-15.**

Ratchet. A gear milled with teeth and mounted at the back of the cylinder of a revolver which engages the pawl that turns the cylinder.

Revolver. Short for 'revolving pistol.' Used today to describe any cylinder-revolving handgun.

Rifle. Technically, any firearm whose barrel is grooved, or 'rifled,' on the inside, thus causing the bullet to spin as it is fired. Rifles were invented in Europe in the 16th century and adapted to American use in the early-to-middle 1700s. The Kentucky Rifle is the most famous adaption of the earlier European versions.

Rifling. The particular pattern of grooving on the inside of a barrel which imparts lateral spin to the bullet, thus increasing accuracy by means of gyroscopic force.

Rimfire. A metallic cartridge whose percussion priming mechanism is in the rim, rather than the center, of the cartridge base.

Shot. *(see Bullet)*

Shotgun. A smoothbore gun, made to discharge either shot or a large, soft, hollow 'slug.'

Sight. A device, composed of two parts, used for aiming a weapon. These two parts are: a notch or more sophisticated device at the breech of the barrel and a blade, pin or ball at the muzzle of the barrel.

Single Action. A type of revolver action in which the hammer must be cocked by hand before the trigger can cause it to fall on the charge. The manual cocking of the hammer rotates the cylinder and, therefore, the cartridge into its proper position.

Trigger. A lever which, when pulled upon by the finger, engages the firing mechanism of the firearm.

Triggerguard. Generally, a loop of metal surrounding the trigger which prevents its being accidentally struck.

Wheellock. This was the first type of ignition for a firearm that did not require a lighted match to set off the powder. The mechanism was actually a windable, spring-loaded wheel which struck sparks against a piece of flint, thus igniting the weapon's powder charge.

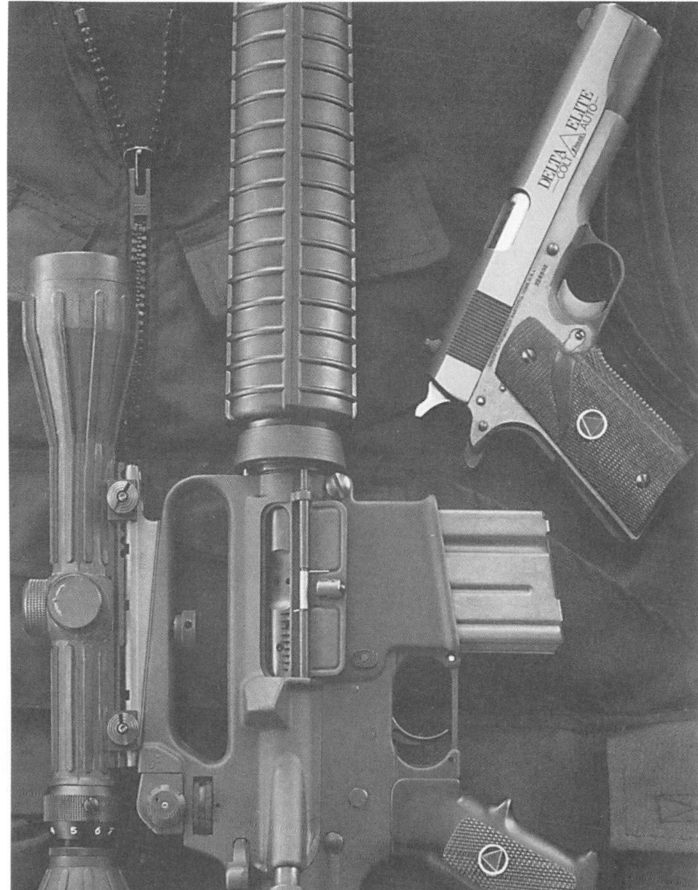

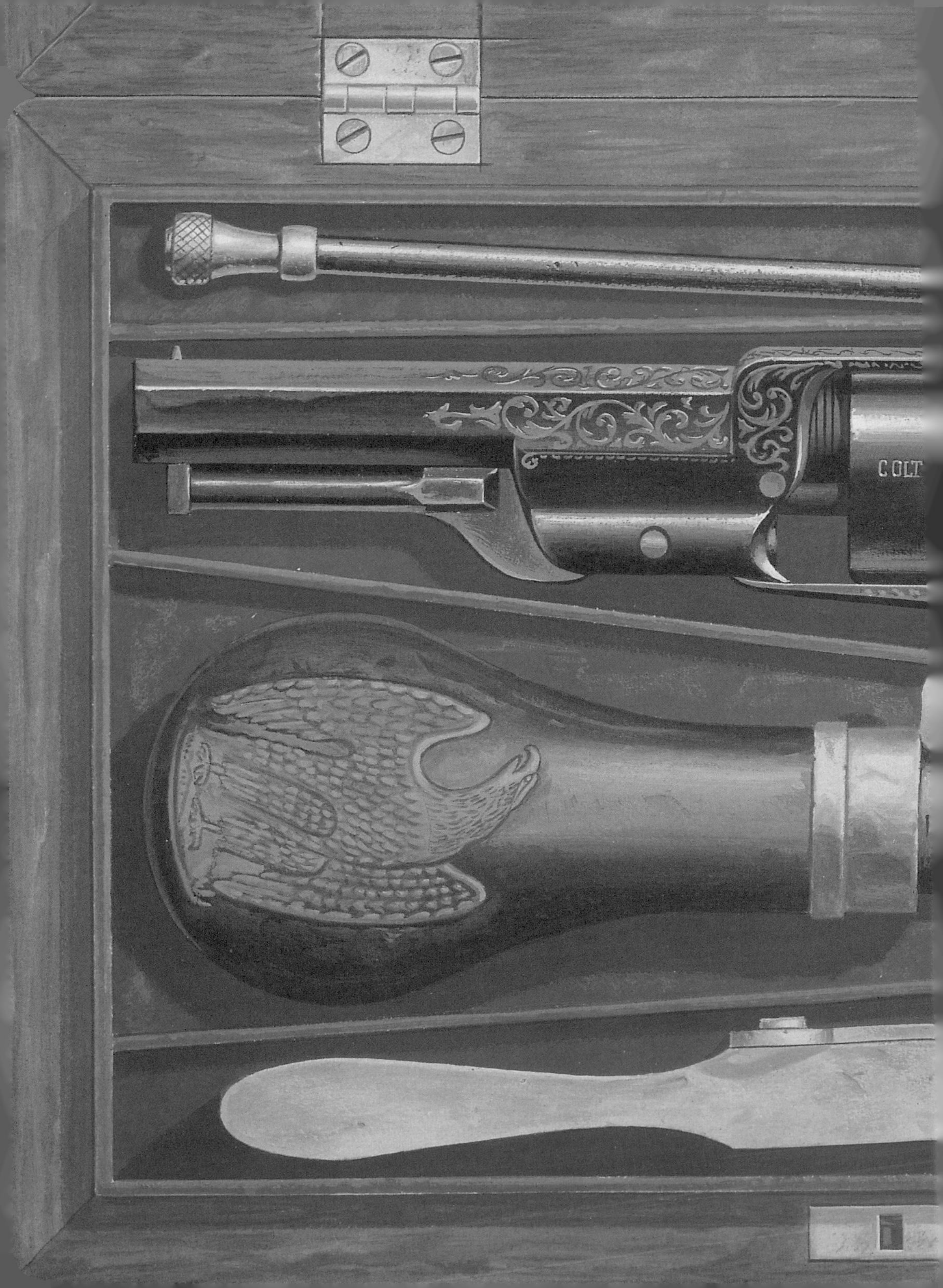
COLT

Above: A fine-grade New Pocket Pistol, circa 1855, in presentation case with bullet mold, powder flask and all the trimmings. Samuel Colt invented the concept of factory-made presentation grade firearms to publicly promote his own factory's precision operations.

Index